SpringerBriefs in Finance

More information about this series at http://www.springer.com/series/10282

Kuo-Ping Chang

The Ownership of the Firm, Corporate Finance, and Derivatives

Some Critical Thinking

Springer

Kuo-Ping Chang
National Tsing Hua University
Hsinchu City
Taiwan

ISSN 2193-1720 ISSN 2193-1739 (electronic)
SpringerBriefs in Finance
ISBN 978-981-287-352-1 ISBN 978-981-287-353-8 (eBook)
DOI 10.1007/978-981-287-353-8

Library of Congress Control Number: 2014956219

Springer Singapore Heidelberg New York Dordrecht London

Printed on acid-free paper

Springer Science+Business Media Singapore Pte Ltd. is part of Springer Science+Business Media (www.springer.com)

All truths are easy to understand once discovered; the point is to discover them.

Galileo Galilei

To Lijing, Wanzu and Wanjane

Preface

This book is intended for all those who are interested in the interactions between the theory of the firm, corporate finance, and derivatives. The view in this book is original and challenges the assumptions taken in the seminal papers of financial theory. It offers new perspectives on financial theory, which are enhanced by stories and numerical examples.

The content of this book has evolved from a series of courses I have taught and learned since the early 1980s. It has been a long and lonely journey but I did benefit greatly from interactions with my former students at National Tsing Hua University in Taiwan. I am grateful to all those who have aided the development of this book. Much appreciation goes out to two reviewers for taking their time and providing valuable feedback and comments. Finally, my sincere thanks go to Mr. William Achauer, editor of Springer, for his kind help and encouragement.

Contents

Chapter 1
The Ownership of the Firm

The essence of economics and management is choice (decision-making). Choice is about cost and benefit analysis. For an individual, examine her past behaviors probably can tell what her future strategies and objectives are. But for a group of people, e.g., a firm, it is not easy to understand what the objectives of the firm are, who can determine what, and who should contribute and get what. In this chapter, I use a robber's story to illustrate that there is no such thing as the owner of the gang (firm). Each resource provider has property rights only on the resource he provides, and only those entrepreneurs who can innovate to create excess profits can have the power to control the firm and determine the firm's objectives. When people cooperate, types of contract are determined by the transaction costs of contracting. The transaction costs of contracting are dependent on the contracting parties' risk attitudes. The contracting parties' risk attitudes are dependent on the sizes of their choice sets.

1.1 A Story of Robin Hood

Imagine Robin Hood plans to organize a group of gangsters to rob banks. Here the resource providers are: a planner (the boss: Robin Hood), an archer, a lookout, and an old lady who cooks for the gang. According to the ex-ante contracts among these resources providers, after each robbery, the cook will be the first to get \$2,000, and the rest of the money will be split among the archer (50 %), lookout (30 %), and boss (20 %).[1] After each robbery, the gangsters will hide out for 2–3 months, and redo it again.

Several interesting conclusions can be drawn from this example:

1. *There is no such thing as "the owner of the gang (firm)"*. People organize through voluntary contracts. Each resource provider has property rights only on the resource he provides, i.e., he has an ex-ante choice to join or not to join the firm (gang), and after he invests his resource in the firm (gang), he obtains a

[1] If the cook obtains only \$1,600 this time, she may get compensations (\$400 plus some interests) next time. In any case, it is an ex-ante contract between her and other members of the gang.

K.-P. Chang, *The Ownership of the Firm, Corporate Finance, and Derivatives*, SpringerBriefs in Finance, DOI 10.1007/978-981-287-353-8_1

right to ex-post share the big pie generated by the firm (gang). If it is wrong to say that Robin Hood is the owner of the gang, it is also wrong to say that shareholders are the owners of the firm. Suppose that the gangsters are captured by the authority, all members (including the cook) will be prosecuted since they all are responsible for the "product" they produced. Thus, if a firm's product causes harm to its customers, it will be unfair to hold only the equityholders (the so-called 'owners') responsible and ask them to compensate.[2]

2. *This gang acts like a firm.* The cook is like a debtholder of the gang (the firm): she obtains fixed income, and the archer, lookout and boss are like equityholders: they obtain non-fixed income. After splitting the big pie generated, the resources providers of the firm will put back some resources to continue production. The only difference between a gang and a firm is that the latter does not need to liquidate and hide out for a period of time.[3]
3. *First claim or seniority between stockholders and debtholders is not meaningful.* Although the cook has first claim on the firm's assets and operating income, her first claim does not affect the ex-post distributions among the resource providers. No matter who has first claim (or everyone has the same first claim), the big pie generated ex-post will be split exactly according to the resource providers' ex-ante contracts (i.e., the cook's first claim is meaningless). Also, only in the cases where there are no clear definitions for property rights (such as public goods: fish in a lake owned by no one) can we say that first claim has some advantage. But firms (or gangs) always have clear definitions for the resource providers' property rights, and there is no such thing as: "stockholders do receive more earnings per dollar invested, but they also bear more risk, because they have given lenders first claim on the firm's assets and operating income" (Myers 1984, p. 94).[4]

1.2 Power, Entrepreneur, and Objectives of the Firm

The above discussions seem in line with the contractual theory of the firm, i.e., view the firm as "a nexus of contracts" among participants in the organization. The strongest (and most quoted) statement of the contractarian viewpoint may be found in Alchian and Demsetz (1972, p. 777): "It is common to see the firm characterized by the power to settle issues by fiat, by authority, or by disciplinary action superior

[2] It could be the case that a new stockholder who just bought some shares yesterday.

[3] The gangsters need to hide out because they are unlawful. They are unlawful because they don't pay taxes. An example is Sir Francis Drake, who was considered a hero in England and a pirate in Spain for his raids. On 26 September, 1580, *Golden Hind* sailed into Plymouth with Drake and 59 remaining crew aboard, along with a rich cargo of spices and captured Spanish treasures. Queen Elizabeth appropriated the lion's share of the proceeds. On April 4, 1581, Drake was awarded a knighthood.

[4] I will elaborate more on this important point in Chaps. 3–6.

to that available in the conventional market. This is delusion. The firm does not own all its inputs. It has no power of fiat, no authority, no disciplinary action any different in the slightest degree from ordinary market contracting between any two people". Jensen and Meckling (1976 pp. 310–311) also argue that "the private corporation or firm is simply one form of legal fiction which serves as a nexus for a set of contracting relationships among individuals. ... Viewing the firm as the nexus of a set of contracting relationships among individuals also serves to make it clear that the personalization of the firm implied by asking questions such as 'what should be the objective function of the firm,' or 'does the firm have a social responsibility' is seriously misleading". But this legal fiction (or contractual relations) view of the firm has one problem: Who in the firm has the power to make decisions to direct the resources?

The firm should be more than a nexus of contracts. Otherwise, because we all have contracts with government, each country will become a big "super-firm". Coase (1937, 1960) have pointed out that there are five kinds of transaction costs involved when people interact: the costs of discovering, informing, bargaining, contracting, and monitoring. In the absence of transaction costs, the maximum value of production by the firm or by markets is the same (i.e., the Coase theorem).[5] Coase argues that the size of the firm is determined by two different sets of transaction costs in directing resource allocation: (1) the cost of using the price mechanism (i.e., costs of discovering, informing, bargaining and contracting), and (2) the cost of using authority or power (i.e., monitoring cost). An activity will be included within the firm if its costs of using markets are greater than its costs of using direct authority. However, an activity will not be counted as a part of the firm just because it has a contract with the firm (e.g., outsourcing). It is only when a resource is under the direction of the firm can we say it is a part of the firm. Coase emphasizes the entrepreneur of the firm has the power and authority to direct resources. But Coase has never clearly pointed out where this power or authority comes from. He argues that since the purchaser will not know which of several courses he will want the supplier to take, "the details of what the supplier is expected to do are not stated in the contract but are decided later by the purchaser ... A firm is likely, therefore, to emerge in those cases where a very short-term contract will be unsatisfactory" (Coase 1937, p. 40). That is, in Coase's view, long-term contract gives purchaser the power to direct resources. However, since every resource provider has free choice to join or leave the firm, Coase's long-term contract is, in fact, a short-term contract, and it cannot give the firm (the purchaser) any power.[6]

[5] The Coase theorem emphasizes that "in the absence of transaction costs, there is no economic basis for the existence of the firm ... it does not matter what the law is, since people can always negotiate without cost to acquire, subdivide, and combine rights whenever this would increase the value of production. In such a world the institutions which make up the economic system have neither substance nor purpose" (Coase 1988, p. 14).

[6] Alchian and Demsetz (1972) argue that "it is not true that employees are generally employed on the basis of long-term contractual arrangements any more than on a series of short-term or indefinite length contracts" (p. 784).

I argue that power or authority comes from choices: If you have more choices (i.e., have a larger choice set), you will have more power than the persons you cooperate with. For example, assume that Michael Jordan is the only person having special talent in playing basketball, and his five-member basketball team can earn \$70 a year. Other basketball teams, because of having no special talent, can only earn \$50 a year, i.e., each player obtains \$10 opportunity cost. It is clear that the \$20 excess profit (70 − 50 = 20) generated in Michael Jordan's team belongs to Michael Jordan only (because Michael Jordan can cooperate with other players, and other players can earn only \$10 a year). Suppose Michael Jordan takes \$4 from the \$20 excess profit and split it equally among his four other team members (i.e., now each of them can have \$11 a year). Then we can imagine that because Michael Jordan owns the excess profit and can use it to "bribe or buy" people, he will have the power (authority) in his team, and more importantly, his objectives will be the objectives of his team. In the firm, according to Schumpeter's idea, only those entrepreneurs who can innovate and create excess profits (and hence, have more choices and can bribe or buy people) can have power or authority. Other resource providers of the firm can only obtain the opportunity costs of their resources.[7] Once Robin Hood loses his ability to innovate and create excess profits,[8] but his subordinate Little John can, then Little John will replace Robin Hood as the leader of the gang and have the power to direct. An employee currently may be willing to accept a lower pay (in comparison with the opportunity cost he can earn from other employers) if he believes in the future his firm will have a great chance to successfully innovate, and he can have a piece of the possible excess profits.

In sum, the size of the firm is determined by two sets of transaction costs: If monitoring cost is greater than the costs of searching, approaching, bargaining and contracting, the employee (or the department) will be fired, and the firm's size decreases; if monitoring cost is less than other transaction costs, the firm will hire (integrate) people, and the firm's size increases. People may have contracts with the firm but only those who also follow the firm's flexible directions are a part of the firm. Within the firm, the person(s) who is capable of innovating and creating excess profits has the power to direct resources, and her objectives will be the firm's objectives.

There are several different thoughts of the existence of the firm in the literature.

---

[7] Schumpeter (1934) argues that entrepreneurs are those who can innovate to devise new product, new producing method and new organization structure, and find new markets and new resources. He terms capitalists as the persons who do not innovate but only provide capitals and take risks, and entrepreneurs as the persons who innovate and do not take any risk. Coase, on the other hand, follows Adam Smith and Alfred Marshall's idea that capitalists and entrepreneurs are the same, and entrepreneurs do not have the feature to innovate, i.e., "… I shall use the same term 'entrepreneur' to refer to the person or persons who, in a competitive system, take the place of the price mechanism in the direction of resources" (Coase 1937, footnote 10, p. 36).

[8] Sociologists may call it: lose charisma, and management professionals may call it: lose leadership.

Alchian and Demsetz (1972) use three factors to explain the existence of the firm. First, because of shirking in the team production of the firm, a monitor is needed to detect and determine each individual's contribution to the output of the cooperating inputs. The monitor, as a residual claimant, earns the net earnings of the team (i.e., net of payments to other inputs) through the reduction of shirking. Second, "to discipline team members and reduce shirking, the residual claimant must have power to revise the contract terms and incentives of *individual* members without having to terminate or alter every other input's contract" (p. 782).[9] Third, "how can residual-claimant, central-employer-owner, demonstrate ability to pay the other hired inputs the promised amount in the event of loss? He can pay in advance or he can commit wealth sufficient to cover negative residuals. The latter can take the form of machines, land, buildings, or raw materials committed to the firm" (p. 791). I will argue that, first, just like other input providers, Alchian et al.'s monitor is also an input provider of the firm. Unlike Marxist's capitalist, Alchian et al.'s monitor does not have any power to pressure labors (and other resource providers) to work harder and exploit them to receive the residual since each resource provider (including the monitor) can freely choose to leave or stay in the firm. Second, whether the firm will make contracts with new or additional suppliers is not the resource providers' concern because they have free choice to leave or stay and only care whether they can earn the opportunity costs of the resources they have provided. The monitor will not have any power just because he can make new contracts or revise or terminate old contracts.[10] Third, the monitor will not have the power because "he can pay in advance or he can commit wealth sufficient to cover negative residuals". The monitor will have the power (or authority) to direct only when he is a Schumpeterian entrepreneur who can innovate and create excess profits (to buy or bribe people).

Hart (1995) argues that "the concept of nonhuman assets is also helpful in clarifying the notion of authority ... Coase ... argued that the distinguishing feature of the employer-employee relationship is that an employer can tell an employee what to do ... When nonhuman assets are present, it is not difficult to understand the difference between the employer-employee situation and the independent contractor situation. In the former case, if the relationship breaks down, the employer walks away with all the nonhuman assets, whereas in the latter case each independent contractor walks away with some nonhuman assets. This difference gives

---

9 This view point is similar to Coase's (1937) argument: "It is true that contracts are not eliminated when there is a firm, but they are greatly reduced. A factor of production (or the owner thereof) does not have to make a series of contracts with the factors with whom he is co-operating within the firm, as would be necessary, of course, if this co-operation were a direct result of the working of the price mechanism" (p. 39).

10 Contrary to Coase's argument, producing by markets might also not need to make a series of contracts. For example, a merchant makes contracts with different firms (labors) to manufacture different parts of a machine, and then organizes these parts to make the machine (i.e., it is a kind of outsourcing). These firms (labors) will only care about the opportunity costs they can earn, and do not need to make contracts with each other. In this case, the merchant (the 'organizer') will not have any power (since everything will be done according to well-specified ex-ante contracts).

the employer leverage" (pp. 57–58).[11] But again, as long as the so-called 'employee' can innovate to create excess profits, he will have the power and can "fire the employer" and cooperate with others. Nonhuman assets (such as machines, land or money) do not provide authority or leverage.

Alchian and Woodward (1987, 1988) propose that within the firm, team members have some specific knowledge, and departure of part of the team can threaten the team's value. Members will want assurance of performance and compensation before they will be willing to make any self-financed investments in the team's efforts (hence, long-term contracts and teamwork co-exist). Alchian and Woodward also argue that team members who own resources (human as well) whose values depend most heavily on the performance of the team (i.e., are the most team-specific) will be willing to pay the most for the right to control the team and own the residual value.[12] The team members, whose resource values most dependent on the performance of the team, are "the directors, administrators and managers (or their principals) of the team's activities, and by convention, are called the 'owners of the firm'".[13] Williamson (1988) emphasizes credible commitments (not credible threats) as a protection from post-contractual opportunism (shirking). He concludes that whether labor serves on the board of directors depends on whether employees have made firm-specific investments (e.g., develop skills or knowledge with firm-specific value). It is interesting to note, however, that even in human's smallest organization-marriage, "long-term contract" and "credible commitments" don't seem plausible.

Berle and Means (1932) argue that dispersed owners of the modem corporation do not have the incentive to effectively control corporate management—directors and officers—and that managers often act in their own interests rather than in the stockholders' interests (hence, a rise in the power of managers). Williamson (1975) suggests hierarchy in organizations may mitigate the problem of controlling opportunism. Holmstrom (1979) and Grossman and Hart (1983) argue that the least easily monitored agent (i.e., the manager) whose effort makes the most difference to output should be the residual claimant. Fama and Jensen (1983) claim that in large open corporations, agency problems arise when the decision managers who initiate and implement important decisions are not the major residual claimants and therefore do not bear a major share of the wealth effects of their decisions. Fama and Jensen propose to control the agency problems by separating the management

---

[11] Rajan and Zingales (1998) also argue that the person who has the ability to grant, deny, or terminate access to the firm's productive assets has power.

[12] Klein et al. (1978) suggest that the "monitoring the monitors" problem may be solved by making the owners of the most firm-specific assets the residual claimants.

[13] Some law professionals (e.g., O'Kelley 2012) argue that the corporation is a by-product of contractual bargaining between a subset of the firm's constituents who voluntarily choose to organize their business relationship by forming a corporation and agreeing to act as the corporation's officers, directors and shareholders. Corporation law assigns to the corporation the role of sole-proprietor-surrogate. The sole proprietor possesses a position within the firm and a bundle of property rights which are generally described as the powers and position of an owner.

(initiation and implementation) and control (ratification and monitoring) of decisions. In sum, hierarchy or the separation of management and control decisions in large organizations can be used to mitigate agency problems in ex-post operations. But the powers to determine the firm's (ex-ante) objectives are still in the hands of innovative entrepreneurs.

1.3 Choice, Risk Attitude, and Types of Contract

In the modern economy, under private ownership of resources, the contracting parties can freely choose among different contracts: a wage contract, a fixed-rent contract, a share contract, or a combination of each. Cheung (1969) suggests that the choice of contracts is determined by weighing the gains from risk dispersions and the costs of contracting associated with different contracts. He argues that "given the transaction cost, risk aversion implies that asset values and the variances of income are negatively related. While in itself the dispersion of risk under a share contract will lead to higher values for the contracted resources, the higher associated transaction cost will lead to lower asset values" (p. 27).

I argue that the transaction costs of contracting are dependent on the contracting parties' risk attitudes, and the contracting parties' risk attitudes are dependent on the sizes of their choice sets. For example, if a person doesn't have much saving and his spouse is not working, then we say this person has a smaller choice set and is risk averse in the sense that he needs to choose a wage (fixed payment) contract and cannot choose a share (uncertain payment) contract. If on the other hand, a person who has wealth and, hence, can choose a wage, a fixed-rent, or a share contract, then he is termed as having a larger choice set and is less risk averse. The transaction costs of contracting will be prohibitively high if all contracting parties want a wage contract (i.e., all have smaller choice sets). The costs of contracting will be lower if one of the contracting parties has a larger choice set (less risk averse), and can take an uncertain payment contract.[14]

Cheung (1969) reports that in China, share tenancy appears more frequent in the wheat region than in the rice region, and higher proportional variances for wheat than for rice. He suggests that share rent is generally slightly higher than fixed (crop) rent, and this premium may be regarded as a return for risk bearing to the landowner. I will argue that higher share rent may be due to the fact that tenants in the wheat regions have less choices: In China's north (wheat) region, tenants are much poorer because except farming they cannot find much work to do (and the landowners can charge "monopolistic rents"); whereas in the south (rice) region

[14] Still, it is the entrepreneur who innovates to earn excess profits can have the power to direct even if she has no wealth and needs a wage (or a mixed) contract: "One entrepreneur may sell his service to another for a certain sum of money, while the payment to his employees may be mainly or wholly a share in profits" (Coase, 1937, p. 41).

with a more prosperous economy, tenants can also work in other jobs (e.g., owning small workshops) and hence, can choose the fixed-rent contract. Atack and Passell (1996) also find that after the American Civil War, former slaves in the south still worked for their previous masters with "dependent" share contracts. This is because the newly liberated slaves didn't have other job opportunities—labor markets were closed to them then, and they still needed protections from their previous masters.[15]

In the modern public firm, the relationship between equityholder and debtholder is like a wage or a fixed-rent contract: the equityholder is like a landowner, and the debtholder is like a tenant. Manager and equityholder seem to have a share contract. With a big middle class, capital markets can gather large capital from people who have small amount of wealth. Limited liability also helps lower the transaction costs of investing: If shareholders were liable for debts of the firm, both creditors and shareholders would need to investigate the wealth of each shareholder. But limited liability is not only limited to stock. All the resource providers in the firm (shareholders, bondholders, material providers and workers) have limited liability. Also, whether a resource provider's rights can be transferred or sold to other investors depends on whether the service provided by the resource is homogeneous. For example, in the previous Robin Hood's story, all the gangsters (including the cook) have limited liability, but they cannot sell their rights to outsiders unless other members of the gang agree. However, if there is a capitalist who provides the gang weapons (capitals), then this capitalist's rights can be transferred to another capitalist without the agreement from other members.

References

Alchian A, Demsetz H (1972) Production, information costs, and economic organization. Am Econ Rev 62:777–795

Alchian A, Woodward S (1987) Reflections on the theory of the firm. J Inst Theor Econ 143:110–136

Alchian A, Woodward S (1988) The firm is dead; long live the firm: a review of Oliver E. Williamson's the economic institutions of capitalism. J Econ Lit 26:65–79

Atack J, Passell P (1996) A new economic view of American history (Chaps. 12 and 14). W.W. Norton Company, New York

Berle, A, Means G (1932) The modern corporation and private property. Harcourt, Brace & World, Inc., New York

Cheung S (1969) The theory of share tenancy. The University of Chicago Press, Chicago

Coase R (1937) The nature of the firm. Economica 4:386–405; also in Coase R (ed) (1988) The firm, the market and the law. The University of Chicago Press, Chicago, pp 33–55

Coase R (1960) The problem of social cost. J Law Econ 3:1–44; also in Coase R (ed) (1988) The firm, the market and the law. The University of Chicago Press, Chicago, pp 95–156

Coase R (1988) The firm, the market and the law. The University of Chicago Press, Chicago

Fama E, Michael J (1983) Agency problems and residual claims. J Law Econ 26:327–349

[15] In a complete market with no transaction costs and no arbitrage, all types of labor contract have the same value. See Proposition 5.2 in Chap. 5.

Grossman S, Hart O (1983) Unemployment with observable aggregate shocks. J Polit Econ 91:907–928
Hart O (1995) Firms, contracts and financial structure. The Oxford University Press, Oxford
Holmström B (1979) Moral hazard and observability. Bell J Econ 10:74–91
Jensen M, Meckling W (1976) Theory of the firm: managerial behavior, agency costs and ownership structure. J Financ Econ 3:305–360
Klein B, Crawford RG, Alchian A (1978) Vertical integration, appropriable rents, and the competitive contracting process. J Law Econ 21:297–326
Myers S (1984) The search for optimal capital structure. Midl Corp Financ J 1:6–16; also in Stern JM, Chew DH Jr (ed) (1986) The revolution in corporate finance. Basil Blackwell, Oxford, pp 91–99
O'Kelley Charles (2012) Coase, Knight, and the nexus-of-contracts theory of the firm: a reflection on reification, reality, and the corporation as entrepreneur surrogate. Seattle Univ Law Rev 35:1247–1269
Rajan R, Zingales L (1998) Power in a theory of the firm. Quart J Econ 113:387–432
Schumpeter J (1934) The theory of economic development: an inquiry into profits, capital, credit, interest, and the business cycle. Harvard University Press, Cambridge
Williamson OE (1975) Markets and hierarchies: analysis and antitrust implication: a study in the economics of internal organization. Free Press, New York
Williamson OE (1988) The logic of economic organization. J Law Econ Organ 4:65–93

Chapter 2
Maximizing Profits and Maximizing Resource Providers' Wealth

In microeconomics, the firm is set to maximize excess profits. In corporate finance, the firm is supposed to maximize shareholders' wealth. Some even argue that the firm should maximize stakeholders' wealth. In this chapter, I show that under certainty with no transaction costs, maximizing excess profits, maximizing shareholders' wealth and maximizing stakeholders' wealth are equivalent. Modigliani and Miller's (1958) capital structure irrelevancy proposition is a restatement of the Coase theorem. With fixed investment, higher debt brings higher rate of return on equity but brings no risk to the equityholder.

2.1 The Coase Theorem and the Modigliani-Miller Propositions

Assume a one-period model: In the beginning of the period, the firm employs labor (L) and capital (K) to produce output ($q = q(L, K)$). At the end of the period, the capital has no scrap value, and the firm sells outputs and liquidates. The firm's profit-maximizing problem is:

$$\underset{L,K}{Max}\ \pi = p(q(L,K)) \cdot q(L,K) - wL - (1+r)K, \tag{2.1}$$

where w is the wage rate, $1 + r$ is the rental price of capital. In Eq. (2.1), a Schumpeterian entrepreneur owns and tries to maximize excess profits, π, by choosing optimal labor and capital inputs. The resource providers: the labor and the capitalist can only earn opportunity costs: w and $1 + r$, respectively.

The first-order conditions for Eq. (2.1) are:

$$\frac{\partial \pi}{\partial K} = \frac{\partial}{\partial K}[p(q(L,K)) \cdot q(L,K)] - (1+r) \equiv 0 \tag{2.2}$$

$$\frac{\partial \pi}{\partial L} = \frac{\partial}{\partial L}[p(q(L,K)) \cdot q(L,K)] - w \equiv 0. \tag{2.3}$$

K.-P. Chang, *The Ownership of the Firm, Corporate Finance, and Derivatives*, SpringerBriefs in Finance, DOI 10.1007/978-981-287-353-8_2

From Eq. (2.2) we get $K = K(L, r)$ and from Eq. (2.3), $L = L(K, w)$. The optimal inputs: $L^* = L(r, w)$ and $K^* = K(r, w)$ can be obtained by jointly solving Eqs. (2.2) and (2.3).

We can also use a two-step approach to solve the profit-maximization problem. First, solve Eq. (2.3) for $L = L(K)$, and substitute it into Eq. (2.1):

$$\underset{K}{Max}\ \pi(K) = p(q(L(K), K)) \cdot q(L(K), K) - w \cdot L(K) - (1 + r) \cdot K, \tag{2.4}$$

where "$p(q(L(K), K)) \cdot q(L(K), K) - w \cdot L(K)$" is the capitalist's quasi-rent. Note that deriving $L = L(K)$ from Eq. (2.3) implies that for any given capital K, the capital provider can choose an optimal L to maximize excess profits π. Thus, Eq. (2.4) is the capital provider's wealth-maximizing problem, i.e., it assumes that the capital provider owns the property rights of the production (i.e., in addition to the opportunity costs of the capital input, the capital provider also owns the excess profits). The capitalist chooses optimal capital input K^* to maximize profits by equalizing the marginal revenue (i.e., marginal quasi-rent) with the marginal cost (i.e., the cost of capital):

$$\left.\frac{\partial \pi(K)}{\partial K}\right|_{K=K*} = \left.\frac{\partial [p(q(L(K), K)) \cdot q(L(K), K) - w \cdot L(K)]}{\partial K}\right|_{K=K*} - (1 + r) \equiv 0. \tag{2.5}$$

After deriving the optimal capital input $K^* = K(r, w)$, the optimal labor input $L^* = L(r, w)$ can be calculated from $L = L(K)$. Comparing Eq. (2.1) with Eq. (2.4), we can conclude that in the absence of transaction costs, no matter who (either the capitalist or the entrepreneur) owns the property rights of production (i.e., excess profits) the value of production remains the same.

If on the other hand, we solve Eq. (2.2) first for $K = K(L)$, and then substitute it into Eq. (2.1):

$$\underset{L}{Max}\ \pi(L) = p(q(L, K(L))) \cdot q(L, K(L)) - (1 + r) \cdot K(L) - w \cdot L, \tag{2.6}$$

where "$p(q(L, K(L))) \cdot q(L, K(L)) - (1 + r) \cdot K(L)$" is the labor's quasi-rent. Deriving $K = K(L)$ from Eq. (2.2) implies that for any given L the labor can choose an optimal K to maximize excess profits π. Equation (2.6) is the labor's wealth-maximizing problem, i.e., it assumes that the labor owns the property rights of the production (i.e., in addition to the opportunity costs of the labor input, the labor also owns the excess profits). The labor chooses optimal labor input L^* to maximize profits by equalizing the marginal revenue (marginal quasi-rent) with the marginal cost (the wage rate):

$$\left.\frac{\partial\pi(L)}{\partial L}\right|_{L=L*} = \left.\frac{\partial[p(q(L,K(L)))\cdot q(L,K(L)) - (1+r)\cdot K(L)]}{\partial L}\right|_{L=L*} - w \equiv 0. \quad (2.7)$$

After deriving the optimal labor input $L^* = L(r,w)$, the optimal capital input $K^* = K(r,w)$ can be calculated from $K = K(L)$. Comparing Eq. (2.1) with Eq. (2.6), we conclude that in the absence of transaction costs, no matter who (either the labor or the entrepreneur) owns the property rights of production (i.e., excess profits) the value of production is the same.

In sum, in the absence of transaction costs, maximizing Schumpeterian entrepreneur's excess profits and maximizing any resource provider's wealth are equivalent. For example, assuming in Eq. (2.1), $q(L,K) = L^{1/2}K^{1/2}$, $w = 1$, $r = 0.5625$, and $p(q) = 10 - q$. Solve any of Eqs. (2.1), (2.4) or (2.6), we get the same $\pi^* = 14.0625$, $L^* = 4.6875$, and $K^* = 3$. These are the results of the Coase theorem: in the absence of transaction costs, who (or even no one) owns the property rights of production (excess profits) is irrelevant to the value of production, and "Professor Steven N. S. Cheung has even argued that, if transaction costs are zero, 'the assumption of property rights can be dropped without in the least negating the Coase Theorem' and he is no doubt right" (Coase 1988, pp. 14–15).

In the above example, suppose that the capital provider owns the property rights of the production (i.e., Eq. (2.4)) and invests three units of K of his own money in the production, i.e., no debt. Then the rate of return on equity is: (14.0625 + 3 × 1.5625)/3 = 625 %, and the market value of the firm, i.e., the share which belongs to fund providers, is: 14.0625 + 3 × 1.5625 = 18.75. If the capital provider invests one unit of K of his own money and borrows two units of K from the capital market, then the rate of return on equity increases to: (14.0625 + 1 × 1.5625)/1 = 1,562.5 %, but the market value of the firm is still the same: 14.0625 + 3 × 1.5625 = 18.75.[1] These results show that in the absence of transaction costs, Modigliani-Miller's first proposition (i.e., the market value of the firm is independent of the firm's capital structure) is just the Coase theorem. Also, Modigliani-Miller's second proposition (i.e., the rate of return on equity increases with the firm's debt-equity ratio) holds, but it has nothing to do with risk.

Suppose that the labor provider owns the property rights of the production (i.e., Eq. (2.6)) and invests 4.6875 units of L in the production. Then the rate of return on the labor-owner's input is: (14.0625 + 4.6875 × 1)/4.6875 = 400 %, and the market value of the firm, i.e., the share which belongs to labor providers, is: 14.0625 + 4.6875 × 1 = 18.75. If the labor-owner invests only one unit of L and hires 3.6875 units of L from the labor market, then the rate of return on the labor-owner's input increases to: (14.0625 + 1 × 1)/1 = 1,506.25 %, but the market value

[1] Suppose the capital provider has only one unit of K and decides not to borrow. Then the capitalist's wealth-maximization becomes: $Max_L\ \pi = (10 - L^{1/2}\cdot 1^{1/2})(L^{1/2}\cdot 1^{1/2}) - (1+0.5625)(1) - 1\cdot L$; and $L^* = 6.25$, $K = 1$ and $\pi^* = 10.9375$. The capitalist's wealth is: \$12.5 (=10.9375 + 1.5625) which is less than \$15.625 (= 14.0625 + 1.5625) if she borrows two more units of K from the capital market.

of the firm remains the same: $14.0625 + 4.6875 \times 1 = 18.75$.[2] Thus, if the labor provider owns the property rights of production, we can rewrite the Modigliani-Miller first proposition as: in the absence of transaction costs, the market value of the firm is independent of the ratio of hired labor's input to labor-owner's input, and rewrite the Modigliani-Miller second proposition as: the rate of return on the labor-owner's input increases with the ratio of hired labor's input to labor-owner's input, but it has nothing to do with risk.

2.2 A Simple Example of the Modigliani-Miller Second Proposition

Suppose you have a patent (a particular technology) so that if you invest $8,000 now, you will have $1,200 annually (i.e., rate of return on equity is: 15 % = 1,200/8,000). Banks provide 10 % risk-free interest rate. You will find that if you borrow $4,000 from a bank to invest, the rate of return on equity is: 20 % = 800/4,000. If you borrow $8,000, the rate of return on equity increases to $\infty = 400/0$. This example shows that with fixed investment, higher debt brings higher rate of return on equity but brings no risk to the equityholder.[3]

The above example can be generalized as follows. The cash flow of the levered firm X (i.e., $1,200) belongs to and is distributed to the debtholders and equityholders:

$$X \equiv X_B + X_S \tag{2.8}$$

where X_B is the cash flow for debtholders, and X_S, the cash flow for equityholders. Equation (2.8) is equality by definition. Define $V_L \equiv S_L + B$, $X \equiv (r_{WACC})(S_L + B)$, $X_B \equiv r_B B$, and $X_S \equiv r_S S_L$, where V_L (i.e., $8,000) is the market value of the firm; S_L is the market value of equity; B is the market value of debt; r_{WACC} is the weighted average cost of capital on the levered firm's assets; r_B is the rate of return on debt; and r_S is the rate of return on equity. Equation (2.8) can be rewritten as:

$$(r_{WACC})(S_L + B) \equiv r_B B + r_S S_L, \tag{2.9}$$

---

[2] Suppose the labor provider has only one unit of L and decides not to hire more. Then the labor's wealth-maximization becomes: $Max_K\ \pi = (10 - 1^{1/2} \cdot K^{1/2})(1^{1/2} \cdot K^{1/2}) - (1 + 0.5625)(K) - 1 \cdot (1)$; and $K^* = 3.8072576$, $L = 1$ and $\pi^* = 11.656157$. The labor's wealth is: $12.656157 (= 11.656157 + 1) which is less than $15.0625(=14.0625 + 1) if she hires 3.6875 more units of L from the labor market.

[3] In this case, higher or lower debt will not affect the equityholder's wealth (or welfare). For example, suppose the firm asks the equityholder to withdraw $4,000 from the firm and borrows $4,000 from the money market. Then the equityholder can deposit this $4,000 in a bank, and annually get $400 from the bank and $800 from the firm.

or

$$r_S = r_{WACC} + (B/S_L)(r_{WACC} - r_B). \tag{2.10}$$

The cash flow of the firm, X, is independent of the debt-equity ratio (B/S_L). The firm's value $V_L \equiv S_L + B$ is also independent of the debt-equity ratio. Hence, r_{WACC} must be independent of the debt-equity ratio. The Modigliani-Miller second proposition can thus be derived from Eq. (2.10): As long as r_{WACC} is greater than r_B, increasing debt-equity ratio increases the rate of return on equity. However, increasing debt does not increase any risk to equityholder.

References

Coase R (1988) The firm, the market and the law. The University of Chicago Press, Chicago

Modigliani F, Miller M (1958) The cost of capital, corporation finance and the theory of investment. Am Econ Rev 48:261–297

Chapter 3
A Reconsideration of the Modigliani-Miller Propositions

In their famous and influential article in 1958, Modigliani and Miller present two propositions: First, the market value of any firm is independent of its capital structure, and second, the expected rate of return on the equity of the levered firm increases in proportion to the debt-equity ratio. It is now well-accepted in the finance literature that the Modigliani-Miller first proposition hinges on the assumption that "individuals and corporations can borrow at the same rate" (Modigliani and Miller 1963, p. 437), and the Modigliani-Miller second proposition holds because the equityholders of the levered firm require "a (risk) premium related to financial risk equal to the debt-to-equity ratio times the spread between ρ_k (the expected rate of return on the firm's total assets) and r (the expected rate of return on the debt)" (Modigliani and Miller 1958, p. 271).[1] In this chapter, I show that the Modigliani-Miller first proposition can hold in an economy where there is no capital market for lending and borrowing, and there is no need to assume that individuals and corporations can borrow at the same rate. Also, the Modigliani-Miller first proposition holds regardless of investors' attitudes toward risk, and financial risk (which is the additional risk placed on the equityholders when debt financing is used) plays no role at all in the Modigliani-Miller second proposition.

3.1 A Tale of Two Cows—The Modigliani-Miller First Proposition

Imagine in a barter economy, there is a group of primitive people, and two cows (firms) eat the same food (costs) and produce identical quantities and quality of milk (cash streams). One cow is owned by person A (the sole owner/equityholder). Another cow is "owned" by two persons, B and C. If it is possible, person B can have a certain amount of the milk (the debtholder), and person C takes the rest (the equityholder). Suppose all the people (i.e., the market) think that the cow owned by

---

[1] E.g., Brealey et al. (2013), Brigham and Ehrhardt (2010), Copeland et al. (2004), Levy and Sarnat (1994), Ross et al. (2012), Stiglitz (1969), among others.

K.-P. Chang, *The Ownership of the Firm, Corporate Finance, and Derivatives*, SpringerBriefs in Finance, DOI 10.1007/978-981-287-353-8_3

persons B and C (the levered firm) is more valuable than the cow owned by person A (the unlevered firm), say, persons B and C's cow can exchange for six sheep, and person A's cow can exchange for only five sheep. Then persons B and C can sell their cow for six sheep and buy person A's cow with five sheep. Now, persons B and C own a cow that produces the same quantities and quality of milk and one more sheep. Of course, in equilibrium, the market value of the two cows must be the same (i.e., person A will increase the price of his cow until the prices of the two cows are equal).[2] This simple tale shows that the market value of the firm is independent of its capital structure (i.e., the Modigliani-Miller first proposition), and there is no need to assume that individuals and corporations can borrow at the same rate.[3]

The above proof implicitly assumes that the two cows (firms) operate in a frictionless world (i.e., a world with zero transaction cost: perfect information, no taxes, no bankruptcy costs and no agency costs). Suppose in a frictionless world two firms generate the same perpetual stream of cash flow, $\tilde{X}$, and differ only in their capital structure. If the market value of the levered firm, V_L, is greater than that of the unlevered firm, V_U, then the investors of the levered firm can sell their firm for V_L and buy the unlevered firm with V_U (hence, there is no need to short sell). The investors of the levered firm thus obtain net profits: $\Delta V \equiv V_L - V_U > 0$, and the same cash flow $\tilde{X}$ as before. In equilibrium, V_L must be equal to V_U. Conversely, if $V_U > V_L$, we can use the same argument to reach the conclusion that in equilibrium $V_U = V_L$. With this arbitrage procedure, there is no need to have a capital market for lending and borrowing.[4]

---

[2] A middleman (person D) can also do the arbitrage and get one sheep: Find a person (E) who is willing to pay six sheep for B and C's cow, and buy A's cow with five sheep for B and C, and then do the exchanges among A, B and C, and E simultaneously.

[3] Modigliani and Miller (1958) use the following method to prove their first proposition. Consider two firms generate the same perpetual stream of cash flow, $\tilde{X}$, in each year and differ only in their capital structure. The market value of the unlevered firm is V_U. The market value of the levered firm is $V_L \equiv S_L + B$, where S_L is the market value of equity, and B is the market value of riskless debt. One strategy an investor can take is to buy 15 % of the shares of the levered firm. That is, he invests $0.15S_L$ in the beginning and at the end of each year obtains payoffs $0.15(\tilde{X} - Interest)$. Another strategy is to buy 15 % of the shares of the unlevered firm, and also borrow $0.15B$ from a bank on his own account on the same terms as the firm. That is, the investor invests $0.15(V_U - B)$ in the beginning and at the end of each year obtains payoffs $0.15(\tilde{X} - Interest)$. Since both the strategies produce exactly the same results: $0.15(\tilde{X} - Interest)$, the initial costs of the two strategies must be the same, i.e., $0.15S_L = 0.15(V_U - B)$ or $V_U = V_L \equiv S_L + B$. This kind of proof hinges on the assumption that individuals and corporations can borrow at the same rate (see also Brealey et al. 2003, p. 468; Ross et al. 2010, p. 495).

[4] When all the investors of the levered firm cooperate to do the arbitrage (or there are middlemen), it is no need to sell short and assume equal access (i.e., the types of securities that can be issued by firms can also be issued by investors on personal account, see Fama 1978). If there is only one firm and investors value levered and unlevered firm differently, then the firm can simply change its debt-equity ratio (i.e., a costless window dressing) to benefit its investors.

3.2 Some Fallacious Arguments for the Modigliani-Miller Second Proposition

The Modigliani-Miller first proposition holds for any firm in any market structure (e.g., monopoly or perfect competition), and it has nothing to do with equity-holders' attitude toward risk (i.e., it exists in risk-averse, risk-neutral and risk-love worlds). The cash flow of the levered firm belongs to and is distributed to the debtholders and equityholders. That is,

$$\tilde{X} \equiv \tilde{X}_B + \tilde{X}_S$$

or

$$E(\tilde{X}) \equiv E(\tilde{X}_B) + E(\tilde{X}_S) \tag{3.1}$$

where $\tilde{X}_B$ is the cash flow for debtholders, and $\tilde{X}_S$, the cash flow for equityholders. Note that Eq. (3.1) is equality by definition. Define $V_L \equiv S_L + B$, $E(\tilde{X}) \equiv E(\tilde{r}_{WACC})(S_L + B)$, $E(\tilde{X}_B) \equiv E(\tilde{r}_B)B$ and $E(\tilde{X}_S) \equiv E(\tilde{r}_S)S_L$, where S_L is the market value of equity; B, the market value of debt; $E(\tilde{r}_{WACC})$, the weighted average cost of capital on the levered firm's assets; $E(\tilde{r}_B)$, the expected rate of return on the debt; and $E(\tilde{r}_S)$, the expected rate of return on the equity. Equation (3.1) can be rewritten as

$$E(\tilde{r}_{WACC})(S_L + B) \equiv E(\tilde{r}_B)B + E(\tilde{r}_S)S_L, \tag{3.2}$$

or

$$E(\tilde{r}_S) = E(\tilde{r}_{WACC}) + (B/S_L)[E(\tilde{r}_{WACC}) - E(\tilde{r}_B)]. \tag{3.3}$$

The expected cash flow of the firm $E(\tilde{X})$ is assumed to be independent of the debt-equity ratio (B/S_L). The firm's value V_L by the Modigliani-Miller first proposition is independent of the debt-equity ratio. Hence, $E(\tilde{r}_{WACC})$ must be independent of the debt-equity ratio. The Modigliani-Miller second proposition can thus be derived from Eq. (3.3): As long as $E(\tilde{r}_{WACC})$ is greater than $E(\tilde{r}_B)$, increasing debt-equity ratio increases the cost of equity.

In the finance literature, there are three fallacious arguments for the Modigliani-Miller second proposition:

1. Increasing debt means higher financial risk, and hence, higher expected rate of return on equity.
   The following example can be used to illustrate this argument. A totally equity-financed firm's assets are \$8,000. The firm is considering issuing riskless debt to buy half of the equity, i.e., \$4,000. The interest rate is 10 %. There are two states of nature: expansion and recession, and each has probability 0.5. The outcomes under alternative capital structures are shown in Table 3.1.

Table 3.1 Outcomes under alternative capital structures

	No debt			With debt		
	Recession	Expected	Expansion	Recession	Expected	Expansion
Rate of return on assets (%)	5	15	25	5	15	25
Earnings before interest	\$400	\$1,200	\$2,000	\$400	\$1,200	\$2,000
Interest	0	0	0	\$400	\$400	\$400
Earnings after interest	\$400	\$1,200	\$2,000	0	\$800	\$1,600
Rate of return on equity (%)	5	15	25	0	20	40

From Eq. (3.3), the expected rate of return on the equity after introducing debt can be calculated as: $20\ \% = 15\ \% + (\$4{,}000/\$4{,}000)(15\ \% - 10\ \%)$. Based on this kind of analysis, it is argued in the corporate finance literature that "the use of debt rather than equity funds to finance a given venture may well increase the expected return to the owners, but only at the cost of increased dispersion of the outcomes" (Modigliani and Miller 1958, p. 262); "the levered stockholders have better returns in good times than do unlevered stockholders but have worse returns in bad times, implying greater risk with leverage" (Ross et al. 2012, p. 410); "any gains from using more of what might seem to be cheaper debt capital would thus be offset by correspondingly higher cost of the now riskier equity capital" (Miller 1988, p. 100).[5]

I argue that even in the risk-averse mean-variance world, in any perfectly diversified portfolio it is the covariance and not the variance (or the dispersion) of rate of return termed as the measure for risk. The increase in the variance of rate of return on equity has little impact on the increase of cost of equity.[6]

5 Equation (3.3) can be written as:

$$\tilde{r}_S = \tilde{r}_{WACC} + (\frac{B}{S_L})(\tilde{r}_{WACC} - \tilde{r}_B) = (1 + \frac{B}{S_L}) \cdot \tilde{r}_{WACC} - (\frac{B}{S_L}) \cdot \tilde{r}_B,$$

where $\tilde{r}_{WACC} = \tilde{X}/(S_L + B)$. Suppose debt is riskless, i.e., $\tilde{r}_B \equiv r_B$. Then the variance of the rate of return on equity is:

$$Var(\tilde{r}_S) = (1 + \frac{B}{S_L})^2 \cdot Var(\tilde{r}_{WACC}).$$

Since the Modigliani-Miller first proposition holds, changes in the debt-equity ratio (B/S_L) will not affect the firm's value $(S_L + B)$, and the probability density function of $\tilde{r}_{WACC}$ (and $Var(\tilde{r}_{WACC})$) does not change. Thus, when the debt-equity ratio increases, the variance of the rate of return on equity will also increase.

6 See also Proposition 5.1 in Chap. 5.

2. From the capital asset pricing model (CAPM), it is found that higher debt means higher beta of equity and, hence, higher expected rate of return on equity. Suppose the CAPM holds. The expected rates of return on debt and equity can be shown as:

$$E[\tilde{r}_S] = R_f + (E[\tilde{R}_M] - R_f) \cdot \beta_S \tag{3.4}$$

$$E[\tilde{r}_B] = R_f + (E[\tilde{R}_M] - R_f) \cdot \beta_B \tag{3.5}$$

Multiply both sides of Eq. (3.4) by S_L, and multiply both sides of Eq. (3.5) by B, and then add them up:

$$\begin{aligned} E[\tilde{r}_{WACC}] \cdot (S_L + B) &\equiv E[\tilde{r}_S] \cdot S_L + E[\tilde{r}_B] \cdot B \\ &= R_f(S_L + B) + (E[\tilde{R}_M] - R_f) \cdot (\beta_S S_L + \beta_B B), \end{aligned}$$

or

$$E[\tilde{r}_{WACC}] = R_f + (E[\tilde{R}_M] - R_f) \cdot (\beta_S \frac{S_L}{S_L + B} + \beta_B \frac{B}{S_L + B}). \tag{3.6}$$

Define

$$\beta_{WACC} = \beta_S \frac{S_L}{S_L + B} + \beta_B \frac{B}{S_L + B},$$

then

$$\beta_S = \beta_{WACC} + (\frac{B}{S_L}) \cdot (\beta_{WACC} - \beta_B). \tag{3.7}$$

Hamada (1969) (see also Brealey et al. 2010, p. 428) argues that when the Modigliani-Miller first proposition holds, the changes in debt-equity ratio (B/S_L) will not affect the value of $E[\tilde{r}_{WACC}]$ (where $E[\tilde{r}_{WACC}] \equiv E[\tilde{X}]/(S_L + B)$) or the value of β_{WACC} [from Eq. (3.6)]. If the debt is riskless (i.e., $\beta_B = 0$), then from Eq. (3.7), it is found that increasing debt-equity ratio (B/S_L) will increase the beta of equity (β_S), and hence, the expected rate of return on equity $E[\tilde{r}_S]$ of Eq. (3.4) will increase.

I argue that the above proof is a tautology. If we want to conclude from Eq. (3.7) that increasing debt-equity ratio (B/S_L) increases the beta of equity (β_S), we will have to assume that β_{WACC} is greater than β_B. But assuming that β_{WACC} is greater than β_B is equivalent to assuming that $E[\tilde{r}_{WACC}]$ of Eq. (3.6) is greater than $E[\tilde{r}_B]$ of Eq. (3.5). From Eq. (3.3), we already know that if the Modigliani-Miller first proposition holds and $E[\tilde{r}_{WACC}]$ is greater than $E[\tilde{r}_B]$, increasing debt-equity ratio will increase the cost of equity, and whether the CAPM or any other asset pricing models hold is irrelevant.

3. "Stockholders do receive more earnings per dollar invested, but they also bear more risk, because they have given lenders first claim on the firm's assets and operating income" (Myers 1984, p. 94).
   This is an incorrect statement since debtholders' first claim will not affect equityholders' wealth (or welfare). For example, in Table 3.1, if the firm asks equityholders to withdraw $4,000 from the firm and replaces that part of equity with debt, the equityholders can (with 10 % riskless rate of return) invest this $4,000 into the money market and/or to buy the bonds issued by the firm (if they cannot do this, there will be no change in the capital structure). The equityholders can still obtain the same stream of the cash flow and 15 % expected rate of return as they do in the totally equity-financed case. We can also think in this way: Even before changing the firm's capital structure, half of the equityholders' investment (i.e., $4,000) is already paid 20 % expected rate of return, and the other half ($4,000), 10 % certain rate of return. It is not the so-called first claim of the debtholders that makes the equityholders have 20 % expected rate of return on $4,000 equity.

References

Brealey R, Myers S, Allen F (2003) Principles of corporate finance. McGraw-Hill, New York
Brealey R, Myers S, Allen F (2010) Principles of corporate finance. McGraw-Hill, New York
Brealey R, Myers S, Allen F (2013) Principles of corporate finance. McGraw-Hill, New York
Brigham E, Ehrhardt M (2010) Financial management: theory and practice. South-Western College Publisher, New York
Copeland T, Weston JF, Shastri K (2004) Financial theory and corporate policy. Prentice Hall, New York
Fama E (1978) The effect of a firm's investment and financing decisions on the welfare of its security holders. Am Econ Rev 68:272–284
Hamada RS (1969) Portfolio analysis, market equilibrium and corporation finance. J Financ 24:13–31
Levy H, Sarnat M (1994) Capital investment and financial decisions. Prentice Hall, New York
Miller M (1988) The Modigliani-Miller propositions: after thirty years. J Econ Perspect 2:99–120
Modigliani F, Miller M (1958) The cost of capital, corporation finance and the theory of investment. Am Econ Rev 48:261–297
Modigliani F, Miller M (1963) Corporate income taxes and the cost of capital: a correction. Am Econ Rev 53:433–443
Myers S (1984) The search for optimal capital structure. Midl Corp Financ J 1:6–16; also in Stern JM, Chew DH Jr (eds) (1986) The revolution in corporate finance. Basil Blackwell, Oxford, pp 91–99
Ross S, Westerfield R, Jaffe J (2010) Corporate finance. McGraw-Hill, New York
Ross S, Westerfield R, Jaffe J (2012) Corporate finance. McGraw-Hill, New York
Stiglitz J (1969) A re-examination of the Modigliani-Miller theorem. Am Econ Rev 59:784–793

Chapter 4
Derivatives and the Theory of the Firm

Although various option price properties have been derived under the Black-Scholes-Merton and binomial option pricing models, to date only a few model-free option price properties have been developed in the literature (e.g., Merton 1973). The literature also has not much say about the relationship between derivatives and corporate finance (e.g., Miller 1988). In this chapter, I use simple arbitrage argument to derive a dozen of model-free option price properties. In addition to deriving the Greeks under model-free framework, it is found that first, in contrast to the traditional view, a European call (put) option for a non-dividend-paying asset can also be a European call (put) option for any other non-dividend-paying asset, and every non-dividend-paying asset is also both a European call option and a European put option for any other non-dividend-paying asset. Second, in some cases the time value of the European put option can be negative, and adjust the exercise price of an option can decrease or even erase the time value of the option. Third, the Modigliani-Miller capital structure irrelevancy proposition is a corollary of the put-call parity. Fourth, each of the firm's resource is both a European call option and a European put option, and each resource is a stock plus a forward contract.

4.1 Model-Free Option Prices

In the finance profession, a derivative is defined as a financial instrument whose value depends on, or derives from, the values of another asset (i.e., the underlying asset). A stock option, for example, is a derivative whose value is dependent on the price of a stock. Forward and futures contracts are contracts that both parties are obligated to buy or sell at a future date a given amount of a commodity or an asset at a price agreed on today. Option contracts give a party the right to buy or sell at a future date a given amount of a commodity or an asset at a price agreed on today. To have the right the party must pay a price (i.e., the price of option) to its counterparty.

K.-P. Chang, *The Ownership of the Firm, Corporate Finance, and Derivatives*,
SpringerBriefs in Finance, DOI 10.1007/978-981-287-353-8_4

A call option gives its owner the right to purchase an asset (the underlying asset) for a given price (the exercise or strike price: *K*) on or before a given date (the expiration date: *T*). A put option gives its owner the right to sell an asset for a given price on or before the expiration date. European options can only be exercised on the expiration date. American options can be exercised on or before the expiration date. Because American options have more choices, they are more valuable than European ones.

The following are some important properties of options.

Property 1 *Put-Call Parity for European Call and Put Options.*

Consider two portfolios at $t = 0$, where the underlying asset is one share of a non-dividend-paying stock, and the simple risk-free interest rate between $t = 0$ and $t = T$ is r:

Portfolio A one European call option c with exercise price K, and cash $\frac{K}{1+r}$ deposited in a bank;

Portfolio B one European put option p with exercise price K, and a share of the stock S_0.

On the expiration date $t = T$, both portfolios give exactly the same payoff: $\text{Max}[S_T, K]$. *Thus, the costs of the two portfolios at $t = 0$ must be the same:*

$$c + \frac{K}{1+r} = S_0 + p. \tag{4.1}$$

Equation (4.1) *is called the put-call parity. Suppose* Eq. (4.1) *doesn't hold:*

Case 1: *At $t = 0$, $c + \frac{K}{1+r} > S_0 + p$. Then an investor can immediately get net profit by adopting the following strategy: (i) sell one call and borrow $\frac{K}{1+r}$ from a bank; and (ii) buy one share of the stock and one put option. At $t = T$, if $S_T > K$, the investor obtains zero profit by letting the put option expire, selling the share of the stock to the holder of the call option at the price K, and giving K to the bank. If $S_T < K$, the investor obtains zero profit by exercising the put option and giving K to the bank.*

Case 2: At $t = 0$, $c + \frac{K}{1+r} < S_0 + p$. *Then an investor can immediately get net profit by adopting the following strategy: (i) short-sell one share of the stock and sell one put option; and (ii) buy one call and deposit $\frac{K}{1+r}$ in a bank. At $t = T$, if $S_T < K$, the investor obtains zero profit by using cash K from the bank to exchange for one share of the stock from the holder of the put option, and then give back one share of the stock. If $S_T > K$, the investor obtains zero profit by using cash K from the bank to exercise the call option, and then give back one share of the stock.*

From Eq. (4.1) *it is easy to find that since call and put options are rights, i.e., their values cannot be negative, we have the following lower bounds for European call and put options.*

Property 2 $c \geq S_0 - \frac{K}{1+r}$ *and* $p \geq \frac{K}{1+r} - S_0$.

If at $t = 0$, $c < S_0 - \frac{K}{1+r}$, *then an investor can immediately obtain net profit by short-selling one share of the stock, buying one call option, and depositing cash* $\frac{K}{1+r}$ *in a bank. At* $t = T$, *if* $S_T > K$, *the investor obtains zero profit by using cash K from the bank to exercise the call option, and then give back one share of the stock. If* $S_T < K$, *the investor can obtain net profit:* $K - S_T > 0$ *by getting K from the bank and spending* S_T *to buy one share of the stock from the market, and then giving back that share of the stock.*

If at $t = 0$, $p < \frac{K}{1+r} - S_0$, *then an investor can immediately obtain net profit by borrowing cash* $\frac{K}{1+r}$ *from a bank and buying one share of the stock and one put option. At* $t = T$, *if* $S_T > K$, *the investor can obtain net profit:* $S_T - K > 0$ *by selling that share of the stock for* S_T *and giving K to the bank. If* $S_T < K$, *the investor obtains zero profit by exercising the put option and giving K to the bank.*

Property 3 *An American call option on a non-dividend-paying stock will never be exercised before the expiration date.*

With the same exercise price K and expiration date T, an American call option C is at least as valuable as a European call option c. At $t = \tau = T/2$, Eq. (4.1) *is written as:* $c_\tau + \frac{K}{1+(r/2)} = S_\tau + p_\tau$, *and if* $S_\tau - K > 0$, *we will have* $C_\tau \geq c_\tau \geq S_\tau - \frac{K}{1+(r/2)} > S_\tau - K$, *i.e., the market value of the American call option must be greater than the gain of exercising the call option. For example, suppose that at* $t = 0$, *an issuer issues an American call option with* $K = \$102$. *At* $t = \tau = T/2$, *if the stock price is* $S_\tau = \$105$, *then the American call option's value* C_τ *must be greater than \$3* $(= S_\tau - K)$. *If* C_τ *cannot be sold at a price more than \$3, it will mean that no one (including the seller) in the market believes that the stock price at* $t \in [T/2, T]$ *will be greater than \$105. This is, of course, contradicts the previous assumption that at* $t = \tau = T/2$, $S_\tau = \$105$.[1]

Property 4 *In the put-call parity, if* $c = p$, *then* $K = S_0(1 + r)$, *i.e., the exercise price must equal the underlying asset's forward price.*

For an underlying asset, the relationship between the forward price F_0 *and the spot price* S_0 *is:* $F_0 = S_0(1 + r)$. *For example, suppose at* $t = 0$, $S_0 = \$100$ *and* $r = 2\,\%$. *Then the seller of the forward contract will ask for at least \$102, i.e., she will want:* $F_0 \geq S_0(1 + r)$. *However, the seller cannot sell at a price more than \$102. This is because the buyer of the forward contract can always turn to the spot market to buy one unit of the underlying asset at* $S_0 = \$100$. *Without default, spend \$100 at* $t = 0$ *is equivalent to spend \$102 at* $t = T$.

---

[1] If all investors believe that at $t \in [T/2, T]$, $S_t \leq \$105$, then $S_{T/2} = \$105$ cannot sustain.

Because at $t = T$, *the value of an European call option is:* $\text{Max}[0, S_T - K]$ *and the value of an European put option is:* $\text{Max}[0, K - S_T]$, *at* $t = 0$ *an issuer of European options can increase* K *to decrease* c *and* increase p, i.e., $\frac{\Delta c}{\Delta K} < 0$ (or $\frac{\partial c}{\partial K} < 0$) *and* $\frac{\Delta p}{\Delta K} > 0$ (or $\frac{\partial p}{\partial K} > 0$). *Also,*

Property 5.1 *The difference in the values of two otherwise identical European options cannot be greater than the risk-free-interest-rate-discounted difference in their strike prices, i.e.,* $|\Delta c| < \left|\frac{\Delta K}{1+r}\right|$ *and* $|\Delta p| < \left|\frac{\Delta K}{1+r}\right|$, *where* $\Delta K = K' - K$, $\Delta c = c' - c$ *and* $\Delta p = p' - p$.

From Eq. (4.1), $c + \frac{K}{1+r} = S_0 + p$ *and* $c' + \frac{K'}{1+r} = S_0 + p'$, *we obtain:* $c' - c + \frac{K' - K}{1+r} = p' - p$. *Suppose* $\Delta K = K' - K > 0$. *Then,* $\Delta c = c' - c < 0$ *and* $\Delta p = p' - p > 0$ *which also imply:* $|\Delta c| < \left|\frac{\Delta K}{1+r}\right|$ *and* $|\Delta p| < \left|\frac{\Delta K}{1+r}\right|$.

Note that Eq. (4.1), *the put-call parity, can be used to prove the Modigliani-Miller* (1958) *capital structure irrelevancy proposition (i.e., the market value of the firm is independent of its capital structure). At* $t = 0$, Eq. (4.1) *can be written as* $S_0 = c + \left(\frac{K}{1+r} - p\right)$ *where* S_0 *can be defined as the market value of the levered firm,* c *as the equity of the firm, and* $\left(\frac{K}{1+r} - p\right)$ *as the risky debt of the firm. In the case of riskless debt,* $p = 0$ *and* $S_0 = c + \frac{K}{1+r}$ *where* $\frac{K}{1+r}$ *is the riskless debt. At* $t = T$, *if the equityholders pay* K *to the debtholders, then the equityholders can have the firm,* S_T.[2] *Because debt cannot be negative, we must have:* $\frac{K}{1+r} \geq p \geq 0$ *and hence,* $0 \leq c \leq S_0$. *If at* $t = T$ *the equityholders need to pay more to the debtholders to have the firm (i.e.,* $\Delta K = K' - K > 0$), *then at* $t = 0$, $\Delta c < 0$, $\Delta p > 0$ *and* $0 = S_0 - S_0 = \Delta S_0 = \Delta c + \left(\frac{\Delta K}{1+r} - \Delta p\right)$ *imply: lower equity value, higher debt value, no change in the market value of the firm, and* $\Delta p < \frac{\Delta K}{1+r}$.[3] *This result shows that Modigliani-Miller's capital structure irrelevancy result is a corollary of the put-call parity.*

Property 5.2 $\frac{\Delta c}{\Delta r} > 0$ (or $\frac{\partial c}{\partial r} > 0$) *and* $\frac{\Delta p}{\Delta r} < 0$ (or $\frac{\partial p}{\partial r} < 0$).

(i) *At* $t = 0$, *from* $S_0 = c + \left(\frac{K}{1+r} - p\right)$, *if only* r *increases (* $\Delta r = r' - r > 0$) *and other factors (including* S_0 *and* K) *remain constant, then the firm's debt value will decrease, i.e.,* $\frac{K}{1+r'} - p' < \frac{K}{1+r} - p$, *and* $0 = S_0 - S_0 = c' - c + \left[\left(\frac{K}{1+r'} - \frac{K}{1+r}\right) - (p' - p)\right]$ *implies* $\Delta c = c' - c > 0$ *(i.e., the firm's equity value will increase). Thus,* $\frac{\Delta c}{\Delta r} > 0$.

---

[2] At $t = T$, if $S_T < K$, then the equityholders will not pay K, and the debtholders will have the firm S_T.

[3] Suppose that a person owns both the equity and debt of the firm. Then, pay more or pay less to the debtholder, i.e., the changes of K, will not affect the market value of the firm S_0.

(ii) At $t = 0$ *, for given K and r, riskless debt is:* $\frac{K}{1+r}$, *and risky debt is:* $\frac{K}{1+r} - p \equiv \frac{K}{1+r+\Delta}$ *where* $\Delta > 0$ *is the risk premium. When only r increases* ($\Delta r = r' - r > 0$) *and other factors remain constant, we will have:* $0 > \left(\frac{K}{1+r'} - \frac{K}{1+r}\right) - \left(\frac{K}{1+r'+\Delta} - \frac{K}{1+r+\Delta}\right) = p' - p$. *Thus,* $\frac{\Delta p}{\Delta r} < 0$.

Because $\left(\frac{K}{1+r'} - \frac{K}{1+r}\right) - (p' - p) < (>) 0$, $p' - p < (>) 0$ *and* $c' - c > (<) 0$ *when* $r' - r > (<) 0$, *we will have:* $|\Delta p| < \left|\frac{K}{1+r'} - \frac{K}{1+r}\right|$ *and* $|\Delta c| < \left|\frac{K}{1+r'} - \frac{K}{1+r}\right|$. *Also,* $\frac{\Delta c}{\Delta r} > 0$ *and* $\frac{\Delta p}{\Delta r} < 0$ *imply that changes in r (i.e.,* Δr*) will affect more on the riskless debt than the risky debt.*[4]

Property 5.3 $\frac{\Delta c}{\Delta S_0} > 0$ (or $\frac{\partial c}{\partial S_0} > 0$).

At $t = 0$, *from* $S_0 = c + \left(\frac{K}{1+r} - p\right)$, *suppose only* S_0 *increases* ($\Delta S_0 = S' - S_0 > 0$) *and other factors (including r and K) remain constant. Then* $\Delta S_0 = \Delta c - \Delta p$, *and:*

Case 1: $\Delta c < 0$ *(i.e.,* $\frac{\Delta c}{\Delta S_0} < 0$*) and* $\Delta p > 0$ *(i.e.,* $\frac{\Delta p}{\Delta S_0} > 0$*). This is impossible since* $\Delta S_0 > 0$. *If this case holds, it will mean that increasing the market value of the firm will make both equityholders and debtholders suffered.*

Case 2: $\Delta c < 0$ *(i.e.,* $\frac{\Delta c}{\Delta S_0} < 0$*) and* $\Delta p < 0$ *(i.e.,* $\frac{\Delta p}{\Delta S_0} < 0$*). This means that when* $\Delta S_0 > 0$ *(the market value of the firm increases), the equity value will decrease, the debt value will increase, and there will be some wealth transferring from the equity to the debt. This result is unlikely. Note that when the debt is riskless, i.e.,* $S_0 = c + \frac{K}{1+r}$, $\Delta S_0 > 0$ *only increases the equity value:* $\Delta c = \Delta S_0 > 0$ *and has no effect on the debt. It is implausible that when changing riskless debt to risky debt,* $\Delta S_0 > 0$ *will only benefit debtholders and make equityholders suffered.*

Case 3: $\Delta c > 0$ *(i.e.,* $\frac{\Delta c}{\Delta S_0} > 0$*) and* $\Delta p > 0$ *(i.e.,* $\frac{\Delta p}{\Delta S_0} > 0$*). This means that* $\Delta S_0 > 0$ *will only benefit equityholders and make debtholders suffered.*

Case 4: $\Delta c > 0$ *(i.e.,* $\frac{\Delta c}{\Delta S_0} > 0$*) and* $\Delta p < 0$ *(i.e.,* $\frac{\Delta p}{\Delta S_0} < 0$*). This means that* $\Delta S_0 > 0$ *will benefit both equityholders and debtholders.*

---

[4] Suppose that at $t = T$, a riskless debt will pay K, and a risky debt (if possible) will also pay K. Then, if at $t = 0$, r increases to r', we will have $\left(\frac{K}{1+r'} - \frac{K}{1+r}\right) - \left\{\left(\frac{K}{1+r'} - p'\right) - \left(\frac{K}{1+r} - p\right)\right\} = p' - p < 0$. This is because at $t = T$ if bad economic situations happen, the riskless debt will still be paying K, but the risky debt will be paying less than K, and rising r will make the riskless debtholders lose more money.

Property 5.4 $\frac{\Delta c}{\Delta x} = \frac{\Delta p}{\Delta x}$ *(or* $\frac{\partial c}{\partial x} = \frac{\partial p}{\partial x}$*) for any* $x \notin \{S_0, r, K\}$.

For example, in the Black-Scholes-Merton option pricing model, $\frac{\Delta c}{\Delta \sigma} = \frac{\Delta p}{\Delta \sigma}$ *where* σ *is the volatility. In the binomial option pricing model where* S_0 *could go up to* S_0u $(u > 1)$ *or go down to* S_0d $(0 < d < 1)$, *we have:* $\frac{\Delta c}{\Delta u} = \frac{\Delta p}{\Delta u}$ *and* $\frac{\Delta c}{\Delta d} = \frac{\Delta p}{\Delta d}$.[5]

In the finance literature, the intrinsic value of an option is defined as the maximum of zero and the value the option would have if it were exercised immediately. For a call option, its intrinsic value is $\mathrm{Max}[S - K, 0]$. *For a put option, its intrinsic value is* $\mathrm{Max}[K - S, 0]$. *The time value of an option which arises from the time left to maturity is defined as the difference between option value and intrinsic value. The time value of the European call option is:* $TV^c = c - \mathrm{Max}[S_0 - K, 0]$. *From* Property 2, $c \geq S_0 - \frac{K}{1+r}$ *and hence,* $TV^c \geq 0$. *The time value of the European put option is:* $TV^p = p - \mathrm{Max}[K - S_0, 0]$. *We have the following result:*

Property 6 *Even without changing the expiration dates, issuers of European options can adjust exercise price K to change the time value of European options.*

(i) *For* $S_0 > K$, *if the exercise price increases from K to* K', *i.e.,* $\Delta K = K' - K > 0$, *and* $S_0 > K'$, $\Delta TV^c = TV^{c'} - TV^c = c' - (S_0 - K') - [c - (S_0 - K)] = (c' - c) + (K' - K) = \Delta c + \Delta K > 0$ *and* $\frac{\Delta TV^c}{\Delta K} > 0$; $\Delta TV^p = TV^{p'} - TV^p = p' - p = \Delta p > 0$ *and* $\frac{\Delta TV^{p'}}{\Delta K} > 0$ *because by* Property 5.1, $|\Delta c| < \left|\frac{\Delta K}{1+r}\right|$, *and* $\Delta K > 0$ *implies* $\Delta c < 0$ *and* $\Delta p > 0$.

(ii) *For* $S_0 < K$, *if the exercise price drops from K to* K', *i.e.,* $\Delta K = K' - K < 0$, *and* $S_0 < K'$, $\Delta TV^p = TV^{p'} - TV^p = p' - (K' - S_0) - [p - (K - S_0)] = (p' - p) - (K' - K) = \Delta p - \Delta K > 0$ *and* $\frac{\Delta TV^p}{\Delta K} < 0$; $\Delta TV^c = TV^{c'} - TV^c = c' - c = \Delta c > 0$ *and* $\frac{\Delta TV^c}{\Delta K} < 0$ *because by* Property 5.1, $|\Delta p| < \left|\frac{\Delta K}{1+r}\right|$, *and* $\Delta K < 0$ *implies* $\Delta p < 0$ *and* $\Delta c > 0$.

(iii) *For* $S_0 = K$, *if* $\Delta K = K' - K < 0$, $\Delta TV^c = c' - (S_0 - K') - c = (c' - c) + (K' - K) = \Delta c + \Delta K < 0$ *and* $\frac{\Delta TV^c}{\Delta K} > 0$ *and* $\Delta TV^p = TV^{p'} - TV^p = p' - p = \Delta p < 0$ *and* $\frac{\Delta TV^p}{\Delta K} > 0$; *if* $\Delta K = K' - K > 0$, $\Delta TV^p = p' - (K' - S_0) - p = (p' - p) - (K' - K) = \Delta p - \Delta K < 0$ *and* $\frac{\Delta TV^p}{\Delta K} < 0$, *and* $\Delta TV^c = TV^{c'} - TV^c = c' - c = \Delta c < 0$ *and* $\frac{\Delta TV^c}{\Delta K} < 0$.

Property 7.1 *If in* Eq. (4.1), *K is very small relative to* S_0 *and T is short so that at* $t = T$ *almost surely* $S_T > K$, *then* $p = 0$, *and the European call option price is:* $c = S_0 - \frac{K}{1+r}$.[6]

---

[5] See also Property 5.5.4 in Chap. 5.

[6] Here c is also the value of a forward contract on the non-dividend-paying underlying asset. Suppose there already exists a forward contract with K as its delivery price. Then, the value of this forward contract f at the current time, i.e., at $t = 0$, is $f = (F_0 - K)/(1 + r)$, where F_0 is the forward price if both parties negotiated at the current time. Combine this equation with $F_0 = S_0(1 + r)$, the relationship between the forward price and the spot price, we get $f = S_0 - K/(1 + r)$.

From Property 2, *we know c cannot be less than* $S_0 - \frac{K}{1+r}$. *For example, a firm provides its employees a stock option (a European call option) with* $K = \$10.2$, $S_0 = \$200$, $r = 2\ \%$, *and T is one month. It is very unlikely that after one month, the firm's stock price will be less than \$10.2. Thus, this call option's price at* $t = 0$ *should be:* $c = S_0 - \frac{K}{1+r} = \$190$. *If not, say,* $c = \$191$, *then at* $t = 0$ *an investor can sell one call option* $\frac{\$10.2}{1+2\ \%}$ *from a bank, and buy one share of the stock to earn* $\$1(= 191 + \frac{10.2}{1+2\ \%} - 200)$. *At* $t = T$, $S_T > K$, *say,* $S_T = \$100$, *the holder of the call option will spend \$10.2 to exercise the option, and the investor will obtain zero profit by giving the share of the stock to the holder and paying \$10.2 to the bank.*[7]

For the put option, we have:

Property 7.2 *If in* Eq. (4.1), *K is very big relative to* S_0 *and T is short so that at* $t = T$ *almost surely* $S_T < K$, *then* $c = 0$, *and the European put option price is:* $p = \frac{K}{1+r} - S_0$.

From Property 2, *we know p cannot be less than* $\frac{K}{1+r} - S_0$. *For example, issuing a European put option with* $K = \$204$, $S_0 = \$10$, $r = 2\ \%$, *and T is one month. It is very unlikely that after one month, the stock price will be more than \$204. Thus, the put option's price at* $t = 0$ *should be:* $p = \frac{K}{1+r} - S_0 = \$190$. *If not, say,* $p = \$191$, *then at* $t = 0$ *an investor can sell one put option, short-sell one share of the stock, and deposit* $\frac{\$204}{1+2\ \%}$ *in a bank to earn* $\$1(= 191 + 10 - \frac{204}{1+2\ \%})$. *At* $t = T$, $S_T < K$, *say,* $S_T = \$100$, *the holder of the put option will exercise the option, and the investor will obtain zero profit by transferring \$204 from the bank to the holder and giving back one share of the stock.*

Property 7.3 *From* Properties 7.1 to 7.2, *the Greeks for the European call and put options are:*

$$\frac{\partial c}{\partial S_0} = 1 > 0, \quad \frac{\partial c}{\partial K} = \frac{-1}{1+r} < 0, \quad \frac{\partial c}{\partial r} = \frac{K}{(1+r)^2} > 0,$$
$$\frac{\partial p}{\partial S_0} = -1 < 0, \quad \frac{\partial p}{\partial K} = \frac{1}{1+r} > 0, \quad \frac{\partial p}{\partial r} = \frac{-K}{(1+r)^2} < 0.$$

Property 7.4 *From* Property 7.1, $c = S_0 - \frac{K}{1+r}$, *the time value of the call option is:*

[7] In the Black-Scholes option pricing model, the European call option price is: $c = S_0 \cdot \phi(d_1) - K \cdot e^{-rT} \cdot \phi(d_2)$ where $d_1 = \frac{\ln(\frac{S_0}{K}) + (r + \frac{\sigma^2}{2})T}{\sigma\sqrt{T}}$, $d_2 = d_1 - \sigma\sqrt{T}$.
If $K = \$10.2$, then S_0 needs to be infinite to make $c = S_0 - K \cdot e^{-rT}$.

$$TV^c = c - (S_0 - K) = S_0 - \frac{K}{1+r} - (S_0 - K) = K\left(\frac{r}{1+r}\right) > 0, \quad \text{and}$$
$$\frac{\partial TV^c}{\partial K} = \frac{r}{1+r} > 0.$$

From Property 7.2, $p = \frac{K}{1+r} - S_0$, *the time value of the put option is:*

$$TV^p = p - (K - S_0) = \frac{K}{1+r} - S_0 - (K - S_0) = K\left(\frac{-r}{1+r}\right) < 0, \quad \text{and}$$
$$\frac{\partial TV^p}{\partial K} = \frac{-r}{1+r} < 0.$$

Interestingly, the time value of the European put option is negative.[8] *When K approaches zero, the time value of the call option will disappear, and $C = c = S_0$, i.e., the call is like a transferrable restricted stock. These results and* Property 6 *show that, in addition to time, other factors can also affect the so-called time value of options.*[9]

Property 8

(i) *For any two non-dividend-paying stocks with the same current share price S_0, and the same European call option's exercise price K and expiration date T, suppose K is very small relative to S_0 and T is short so that at $t = T$ almost surely $S_T > K$. Then, these two stocks' call option prices at the current time must be the same: $C = c = S_0 - \frac{K}{1+r}$;*

(ii) *For any two non-dividend-paying stocks with the same current share prices S_0, and the same European put option's exercise price K and expiration date T, suppose K is very big relative to S_0 and T is short so that at $t = T$ almost surely $S_T < K$. Then, these two stocks' put option prices at the current time must be the same: $p = \frac{K}{1+r} - S_0$.*

The above results show that an asset's call or put option can directly be used as another asset's call or put option. This finding challenges the conventional view that an option must be derived from or dependent on some specific underlying asset. Note also that the price behaviours (probability distributions) of the two underlying assets are irrelevant in pricing these options. To price these options all we need are:

---

[8] Since American call and put options can be exercised on or before the expiration date, their time values must be non-negative.

[9] For the multi-period put-call parity, $c + \frac{K}{(1+m)^T} = S_0 + p$ where $t = 0, 1, 2, \ldots, T$, and m is the risk-free interest rate in each period. If K is very small relative to S_0 and T is short so that at $t = T$ almost surely $S_T > K$, then $p = 0$, and the European call option price is: $c = S_0 - \frac{K}{(1+m)^T}$, and $\frac{\partial c}{\partial T} > 0$. If K is very big relative to S_0 and T is short so that at $t = T$ almost surely $S_T < K$, then $c = 0$, and the European put option price is: $p = \frac{K}{(1+m)^T} - S_0$, and $\frac{\partial p}{\partial T} < 0$.

K, r and S_0, where K is determined by the issuers of options, r is determined by the economy, and S_0 is influenced by both the economy and the individual company. This indicates that an asset's current price S_0 may reflect not only the asset's past information but also the market's expectations about the asset's future performance.

Property 9 *If $c = S_0 - \frac{K}{1+r}$ is a European call option for a non-dividend-paying asset, then it can also be a European call option for any other non-dividend-paying asset. If $p = \frac{K}{1+r} - S_0$ is a European put option for a non-dividend-paying asset, then it can also be a European put option for any other non-dividend-paying asset.*

For example, suppose asset A's European call option has K = \$10.2 where $S_0 =$ \$200, $r = 2\ \%$, and T is one month. It is very unlikely that after one month, asset A's unit price will be less than \$10.2. Thus, the call option's price at $t = 0$ is: $c = S_0 - \frac{K}{1+r} =$ \$190. If another asset B's unit price is \$50, then we can let the underlying asset be four units of asset B, and this $c =$ \$190 can also be asset B's call option.

Suppose asset E's European put option has K = \$204 where $S_0 =$ \$10, $r = 2\ \%$, and T is one month. It is very unlikely that after one month, asset E's unit price will be more than \$204. Thus, the put option's price at $t = 0$ is: $p = \frac{K}{1+r} - S_0 =$ \$190. If another asset F's unit price is \$50, then we can let the underlying asset be 0.2 units of asset F, and this $p =$ \$190 can also be asset F's put option.

Property 10 *Every non-dividend-paying asset can be written as a European call option and a European put option for any other non-dividend-paying asset (including itself).*

For example, suppose that for two assets, the first asset's current unit prices is $S_0^1 =$ \$200, and the second asset's current unit price is $S_0^2 =$ \$198. Then S_0^2 can be written as:

(i) *a European call option for one unit of the first asset: $S_0^2 = S_0^1 - \frac{K}{1+r}$, where $K =$ \$2.04, $r = 2\ \%$, and T is one month;*
(ii) *a European put option for one-tenth unit of the first asset: $S_0^2 = \frac{K}{1+r} - (0.1)S_0^1$, where $K =$ \$222.36, $r = 2\ \%$, and T is one month;*
(iii) *a European call option for 1.01 units of the second asset: $S_0^2 = (1.01)S_0^2 - \frac{K}{1+r}$, where $K =$ \$2.0196, $r = 2\ \%$, and T is one month;*
(iv) *a European put option for one-tenth unit of the second asset: $S_0^2 = \frac{K}{1+r} - (0.1)S_0^2$, where $K =$ \$222.156, $r = 2\ \%$, and T is one month.*

4.2 The Firm's Resources and Derivatives

In this section, I show that in the firm, each resource is both a European call option and a European put option, and each resource is a stock plus a forward contract.

4.2.1 Each Resource Is Both a European Call Option and a European Put Option

Assume that in the beginning of the year, the firm is organized by four resource providers: the equityholder provides \$100, the debtholder provides \$200, the material provider provides material which has market value of \$150, and the labor provider provides labor service which has market value of \$50. At the end of the year, the firm liquidates and distributes all it has, $\widetilde{TR}$ (where $\widetilde{TR}$ lies between \$600 and \$1,000), to the four resource providers: the labor provider obtains \$60, the material provider obtains \$180, the debtholder obtains \$240, and the equityholder obtains the residual: Max[0, $\widetilde{TR}$ −480]. That is, in the beginning of the year, the four resource providers exchange their resources for the following rights (options):

	Equity			
	European call		European put	
	(1)	(2)	(1)	(2)
Maturity	One year	One year	One year	One year
Market value of the underlying asset at maturity	Max[0, $\widetilde{TR}$ − 480]	$\widetilde{TR}$	\$0	\$480
Current price of the option	\$100	\$100	\$100	\$100
Exercise price	\$0	\$480	Max[0, $\widetilde{TR}$ − 480]	$\widetilde{TR}$
Payoff of the option at maturity	Max[0, $\widetilde{TR}$ − 480]	Max[0, $\widetilde{TR}$ − 480]	Max[0, $\widetilde{TR}$ − 480]	Max[0, $\widetilde{TR}$ − 480]
	Debt			
	European call		European put	
	(1)	(2)	(1)	(2)
Maturity	One year	One yearr	One year	One year
Market value of the underlying asset at maturity	\$240	$\widetilde{TR}$	\$0	$\widetilde{TR}$ − 240
Current price of the option	\$200	\$200	\$200	\$200
Exercise price	\$0	$\widetilde{TR}$ − 240	\$240	$\widetilde{TR}$
Payoff of the option at maturity	\$240	\$240	\$240	\$240
	Material			
	European call		European put	
	(1)	(2)	(1)	(2)
Maturity	One year	One year	One year	One year
Market value of the underlying asset at maturity	\$180	$\widetilde{TR}$	\$0	$\widetilde{TR}$ − 180

(continued)

(continued)

	Equity			
	European call		European put	
	(1)	(2)	(1)	(2)
Current price of the option	\$150	\$150	\$150	\$150
Exercise price	\$0	$\tilde{TR} - 180$	\$180	$\tilde{TR}$
Payoff of the option at maturity	\$180	\$180	\$180	\$180
	Labor			
	European call		European put	
	(1)	(2)	(1)	(2)
Maturity	One year	One year	One year	One year
Market value of the underlying asset at maturity	\$60	$\tilde{TR}$	\$0	$\tilde{TR} - 60$
Current price of the option	\$50	\$50	\$50	\$50
Exercise price	\$0	$\tilde{TR} - 60$	\$60	$\tilde{TR}$
Payoff of the option at maturity	\$60	\$60	\$60	\$60

Suppose that after the resource providers invested their resources, the firm changes to a more uncertain production activity, and $\tilde{TR}$ after one year will be between \$10 and \$1,600, where according to the corporate law, the labor provider is the first to get payment, the material provider is the second to get payment, the debtholder is the third to get payment, and the equityholder obtains the residual. Then the four resources of the firm are the following European options:

	Equity			
	European call		European put	
	(1)	(2)	(1)	(2)
Maturity	One year	One year	One year	One year
Market value of the underlying asset at maturity	$\text{Max}[0, \tilde{TR} - 480]$	$\tilde{TR}$	\$0	\$480
Current price of the option	\$100	\$100	\$100	\$100
Exercise price	\$0	\$480	$\text{Max}[0, \tilde{TR} - 480]$	$\tilde{TR}$
Payoff of the option at maturity	$\text{Max}[0, \tilde{TR} - 480]$	$\text{Max}[0, \tilde{TR} - 480]$	$\text{Max}[0, \tilde{TR} - 480]$	$\text{Max}[0, \tilde{TR} - 480]$

(continued)

(continued)

	Equity			
	European call		European put	
	(1)	(2)	(1)	(2)
	Debt			
	European call		European put	
	(1)	(2)	(1)	(2)
Maturity	One year	One year	One year	One year
Market value of the underlying asset at maturity	$\$240$ if $TR \geq 480$ $TR - 240$ if $240 < TR < 480$ $\$0$ if $TR \leq 240$	$\tilde{TR}$	$\$0$	$TR - 240$ if $TR \geq 480$ $\$240$ if $240 < TR < 480$ TR if $TR \leq 240$
Current price of the option	$200	$200	$200	$200
Exercise price	$\$0$	$TR - 240$ if $TR \geq 480$ $\$240$ if $240 < TR < 480$ TR if $TR \leq 240$	$\$240$ if $TR \geq 480$ $TR - 240$ if $240 < TR < 480$ $\$0$ if $TR \leq 240$	$\tilde{TR}$
Payoff of the option at maturity	$\$240$ if $TR \geq 480$ $TR - 240$ if $240 < TR < 480$ $\$0$ if $TR \leq 240$	$\$240$ if $TR \geq 480$ $TR - 240$ if $240 < TR < 480$ $\$0$ if $TR \leq 240$	$\$240$ if $TR \geq 480$ $TR - 240$ if $240 < TR < 480$ $\$0$ if $TR \leq 240$	$\$240$ if $TR \geq 480$ $TR - 240$ if $240 < TR < 480$ $\$0$ if $TR \leq 240$
	Material			
	European call		European put	
	(1)	(2)	(1)	(2)
Maturity	One year	One year	One year	One year
Market value of the underlying asset at maturity	$\$180$ if $TR \geq 240$ $TR - 60$ if $60 < TR < 240$ $\$0$ if $TR \leq 60$	$\tilde{TR}$	$\$0$	$TR - 180$ if $TR \geq 240$ $\$60$ if $60 < TR < 240$ TR if $TR \leq 60$
Current price of the option	$150	$150	$150	$150
Exercise price	$\$0$	$TR - 180$ if $TR \geq 240$ $\$60$ if $60 < TR < 240$ TR if $TR \leq 60$	$\$180$ if $TR \geq 240$ $TR - 60$ if $60 < TR < 240$ $\$0$ if $TR \leq 60$	$\tilde{TR}$
Payoff of the option at maturity	$\$180$ if $TR \geq 240$ $TR - 60$ if $60 < TR < 240$ $\$0$ if $TR \leq 60$	$\$180$ if $TR \geq 240$ $TR - 60$ if $60 < TR < 240$ $\$0$ if $TR \leq 60$	$\$180$ if $TR \geq 240$ $TR - 60$ if $60 < TR < 240$ $\$0$ if $TR \leq 60$	$\$180$ if $TR \geq 240$ $TR - 60$ if $60 < TR < 240$ $\$0$ if $TR \leq 60$
	Labor			
	European call		European put	
	(1)	(2)	(1)	(2)
Maturity	One year	One year	One year	One year
Market value of the underlying asset at maturity	$\$60$ if $TR > 60$ TR if $TR \leq 60$	$\tilde{TR}$	$\$0$	$TR - 60$ if $TR > 60$ $\$0$ if $TR \leq 60$

(continued)

(continued)

	Equity			
	European call		European put	
	(1)	(2)	(1)	(2)
Current price of the option	\$50	\$50	\$50	\$50
Exercise price	\$0	$TR - 60$ if $TR > 60$ \$0 if $TR \le 60$	\$60 if $TR > 60$ TR if $TR \le 60$	$\tilde{TR}$
Payoff of the option at maturity	\$60 if $TR > 60$ TR if $TR \le 60$	\$60 if $TR > 60$ TR if $TR \le 60$	\$60 if $TR > 60$ TR if $TR \le 60$	\$60 if $TR > 60$ TR if $TR \le 60$

The above example shows that, first, each resource is a European call option or put option. In the beginning of the year, each resource provider provides his resource to obtain an option (a right) from other resource providers so that, at the end of the year, he can share what the firm has. The firm is fictitious. There is no such thing as "the owner of the firm" since each resource provider has the property rights only on the resource he provides. This result refutes Black and Scholes' (1973) claim that "the bond holders own the company's assets, but they have given options to the stockholders to buy the assets back" (pp. 649–650). Second, when the firm moves from a more certain project (i.e., $\tilde{TR}$ lies between \$600, and \$1,000) to a more uncertain one (i.e., $\tilde{TR}$ lies between \$10 and \$1,600)-higher variance of *TR*, the market value of equity will increase but the market values of debt, material input and labor input will decrease, i.e., there will be a wealth redistribution among the resource providers.[10] This is because the debtholder's, material provider's and labor provider's payments have upper bounds, and they will not benefit if the more uncertain project succeeds but will suffer if the more uncertain project fails. For example, no matter whether the more uncertain project produces $TR = \$800$ or $TR = \$1{,}600$, the debtholder, material provider and labor provider will still obtain the same fixed payments: \$240, \$180, and 60, respectively. But the equityholder will obtain \$320 if $TR = \$800$, and \$1,120 if $TR = \$1{,}600$, i.e., her payment has no upper bound.

4.2.2 Each Resource Is a Stock Plus a Forward Contract

In the above example, in the beginning of the year, the total market value of the four resources is \$500, and the resource providers' shares are: the equityholder (100/500), the debtholder (200/500), the material provider (150/500), and the labor provider (50/500). At the end of the year, if $\tilde{TR}$ is distributed according to the

[10] If the equityholder also suffers losses, the firm will not move to the more uncertain project. See also Example 5.4 in Chap. 5.

resource providers' shares, then all the resource providers are stockholders: the equityholder obtains $\tilde{TR} \times 100/500$, the debtholder obtains $\tilde{TR} \times 200/500$, the material provider obtains $\tilde{TR} \times 150/500$, and the labor provider obtains $\tilde{TR} \times 50/500$. Suppose $\tilde{TR}$ lies between \$10 and \$1,600, and the labor provider wants to have some sure gains instead of $\tilde{TR} \times 50/500$. Then in the beginning of the year, the labor provider can negotiate with the other three resource providers to obtain, say, \$50 plus $(\tilde{TR} - 50) \times 20/500$. That is, the labor provider's right is like a stock which will give $\tilde{TR} \times 50/500$, plus a forward contract which will sell $\tilde{TR} \times 50/500$ for \$50 plus $(\tilde{TR} - 50) \times 20/500$. If the labor provider wants only fixed payment \$60, then his right is equivalent to a stock which will give $\tilde{TR} \times 50/500$ plus a forward contract which will sell $\tilde{TR} \times 50/500$ for \$60. The debtholder's and material provider's rights can also be shown as combinations of stocks and forward contracts. If all the resource providers (including the equityholder) want to have some fixed payments, and the sum of these fixed payments is larger than \$10 (i.e., the minimum value of $\tilde{TR}$), then it will mean that the transaction costs of their cooperation are too high, and the firm cannot exist. Note that although the equityholder receives the uncertain residuals, and the labor provider, debtholder and material provider receive fixed payments, it doesn't mean that the equityholder can have any power or authority in directing the labor provider, debtholder and material provider. This result refutes Knight's (1933) claim that with uncertainty, "the system under which the confident and venturesome 'assume the risk' or 'insure' the doubtful and timid by guaranteeing to the latter a specified income in return for an assignment of actual results ... With human nature as we know it would be impracticable or very unusual for one man to guarantee to another a definite result of the latter's actions without being given power to direct his work. And on the other hand the second party would not place himself under the direction of the first without such a guaranty" (pp. 269–270).[11]

References

Black F, Scholes M (1973) The pricing of options and corporate liabilities. J Polit Econ 81:637–654

Knight F (1933) Risk, uncertainty and profit. Reprinted by the University of Chicago Press, Chicago, 1971

[11] Since each resource is a stock plus a forward contract, it will be meaningless to say that only the equityholder (shareholder) is the owner of the firm, and other resource providers are not. Also, when the firm's product causes damages to its customers, it will be unfair to ask only the equityholder needs to compensate the customers.

Merton R (1973) Theory of rational option pricing. Bell J Econ Manage Sci 4:141–183
Miller M (1988) The Modigliani-Miller propositions: after thirty years. J Econ Perspect 2:99–120
Modigliani F, Miller M (1958) The cost of capital, corporation finance and the theory of investment. Am Econ Rev 48:261–297

Chapter 5
Arbitrage and Valuation of Different Contracts

In this chapter, I first derive the Arbitrage Theorem, and use the theorem to show that, in a complete market with no transaction costs and no arbitrage, all securities or assets are derivatives for each other, and they are dependent on each other. It also shows a capital structure irrelevancy proposition: changes in firms' debt-equity ratios will not affect equityholders' wealth (welfare), and equityholders' preferences toward risk (or variance) are irrelevant. When the firm moves from a more certain project to a more uncertain one, the time-0 price of equity will increase, but the time-0 prices of fixed-income assets will decrease. Different labor contractual arrangements will not affect the time-0 price of labor input. When the firm moves from a more certain project to a more uncertain one, the time-0 price of labor input will increase if it is under the share or the mixed contract.

5.1 The Arbitrage Theorem

Theorem 5.1 *Let S be a nonempty, closed convex set in R^n and $\mathbf{y} \notin S$. Then, there exists a unique point $\overline{\mathbf{x}} \in S$ with minimum distance from $\mathbf{y}$. Also, $\overline{\mathbf{x}}$ is the minimizing point if and only if $(\mathbf{y} - \overline{\mathbf{x}})^t(\mathbf{x} - \overline{\mathbf{x}}) \leq 0$ for all $\mathbf{x} \in S$.*

Proof We first show the existence of a minimum point. Since S is not empty, there exists a point $\hat{\mathbf{x}} \in S$. Define $\overline{S} = S \cap \{\mathbf{x} : \|\mathbf{y} - \mathbf{x}\| \leq \|\mathbf{y} - \hat{\mathbf{x}}\|\}$ and hence, $\inf\{\|\mathbf{y} - \mathbf{x}\| : \mathbf{x} \in S\} = \inf\{\|\mathbf{y} - \mathbf{x}\| : \mathbf{x} \in \overline{S}\}$. Since $\inf\{\|\mathbf{y} - \mathbf{x}\| : \mathbf{x} \in \overline{S}\}$ means finding the minimum of a continuous function over a nonempty, compact set $\overline{S}$, by Weierstrass' theorem, there exists a minimizing point $\overline{\mathbf{x}}$ in S that is closest to the point $\mathbf{y}$.

To show the uniqueness of minimum point, suppose that there is another $\overline{\mathbf{x}}' \in S$ which is also a minimum point, i.e., $\|\mathbf{y} - \overline{\mathbf{x}}'\| = \|\mathbf{y} - \overline{\mathbf{x}}\| \equiv \gamma$. By convexity of S, $(\overline{\mathbf{x}} + \overline{\mathbf{x}}')/2 \in S$. By Schwartz inequality, we get

$$\left\|\mathbf{y} - \frac{\overline{\mathbf{x}} + \overline{\mathbf{x}}'}{2}\right\| \leq \frac{1}{2}\|\mathbf{y} - \overline{\mathbf{x}}\| + \frac{1}{2}\|\mathbf{y} - \overline{\mathbf{x}}'\| = \gamma$$

K.-P. Chang, *The Ownership of the Firm, Corporate Finance, and Derivatives*, SpringerBriefs in Finance, DOI 10.1007/978-981-287-353-8_5

If strict inequality holds, we have a contradiction to $\bar{\mathbf{x}}$ being the closest point to $\mathbf{y}$. Therefore, equality holds, and we must have $\mathbf{y}-\bar{\mathbf{x}}=\lambda(\mathbf{y}-\bar{\mathbf{x}}')$ for some λ. Since $\|\mathbf{y}-\bar{\mathbf{x}}\|=\|\mathbf{y}-\bar{\mathbf{x}}'\|=\gamma$, $|\lambda|=1$. If $\lambda=-1$, then $\mathbf{y}=\frac{\bar{\mathbf{x}}+\bar{\mathbf{x}}'}{2}\in S$ which contradicts the assumption $\mathbf{y}\notin S$. Thus, $\lambda=1$, and we have $\bar{\mathbf{x}}'=\bar{\mathbf{x}}$.

Suppose $(\mathbf{y}-\bar{\mathbf{x}})^t(\mathbf{x}-\bar{\mathbf{x}})\leq 0$ for all $\mathbf{x}\in S$. Then,

$$\|\mathbf{y}-\mathbf{x}\|^2=\|\mathbf{y}-\bar{\mathbf{x}}+\bar{\mathbf{x}}-\mathbf{x}\|^2=\|\mathbf{y}-\bar{\mathbf{x}}\|^2+\|\bar{\mathbf{x}}-\mathbf{x}\|^2+2(\mathbf{y}-\bar{\mathbf{x}})^t(\bar{\mathbf{x}}-\mathbf{x})$$

Since $\|\bar{\mathbf{x}}-\mathbf{x}\|^2\geq 0$ and $(\mathbf{y}-\bar{\mathbf{x}})^t(\bar{\mathbf{x}}-\mathbf{x})\geq 0$ by assumption, $\|\mathbf{y}-\bar{\mathbf{x}}\|^2\leq\|\mathbf{y}-\mathbf{x}\|^2$ for all $\mathbf{x}\in S$, i.e., $\bar{\mathbf{x}}$ is the minimizing point. Conversely, assume that $\bar{\mathbf{x}}$ is the minimizing point. Let $\mathbf{x}\in S$ and $0\leq\alpha\leq 1$. We have $\alpha\mathbf{x}+(1-\alpha)\bar{\mathbf{x}}=\bar{\mathbf{x}}+\alpha(\mathbf{x}-\bar{\mathbf{x}})\in S$ and $\|\mathbf{y}-\bar{\mathbf{x}}-\alpha(\mathbf{x}-\bar{\mathbf{x}})\|^2\geq\|\mathbf{y}-\bar{\mathbf{x}}\|^2$. Therefore, from

$$\|\mathbf{y}-\bar{\mathbf{x}}-\alpha(\mathbf{x}-\bar{\mathbf{x}})\|^2=\|\mathbf{y}-\bar{\mathbf{x}}\|^2+\alpha^2\|\mathbf{x}-\bar{\mathbf{x}}\|^2-2\alpha(\mathbf{y}-\bar{\mathbf{x}})^t(\mathbf{x}-\bar{\mathbf{x}})$$

we can get $2\alpha(\mathbf{y}-\bar{\mathbf{x}})^t(\mathbf{x}-\bar{\mathbf{x}})\leq\alpha^2\|\mathbf{x}-\bar{\mathbf{x}}\|^2$ for all $0\leq\alpha\leq 1$. Dividing this inequality by any such $\alpha>0$ and letting $\alpha\to 0^+$, we have $(\mathbf{y}-\bar{\mathbf{x}})^t(\mathbf{x}-\bar{\mathbf{x}})\leq 0$ for all $\mathbf{x}\in S$.□

Theorem 5.2 (Separating Hyperplane Theorem) *Let S be a nonempty, closed convex set in R^n and $\mathbf{y}\notin S$. Then, there exists a nonzero vector $\mathbf{z}\in R^n$ and a scalar α such that $\mathbf{z}^t\mathbf{y}<\alpha$ and $\mathbf{z}^t\mathbf{x}\geq\alpha$ for each $\mathbf{x}\in S$.*

Proof From Theorem 5.1 we know that because the set S is a nonempty, closed convex set in R^n and $\mathbf{y}\notin S$, there exists a unique minimizing point $\bar{\mathbf{x}}$ that $(\mathbf{y}-\bar{\mathbf{x}})^t(\mathbf{x}-\bar{\mathbf{x}})\leq 0$ for all $\mathbf{x}\in S$.

Letting $\mathbf{z}=-(\mathbf{y}-\bar{\mathbf{x}})$ and $\alpha=\mathbf{z}^t\bar{\mathbf{x}}$, we have $\mathbf{z}^t(\mathbf{x}-\bar{\mathbf{x}})\geq 0$ and hence, $\mathbf{z}^t\mathbf{x}\geq\alpha$ for each $\mathbf{x}\in S$. Also, $\mathbf{z}^t\mathbf{y}-\alpha=\mathbf{z}^t(\mathbf{y}-\bar{\mathbf{x}})=-(\mathbf{y}-\bar{\mathbf{x}})^t(\mathbf{y}-\bar{\mathbf{x}})<0$ or $\mathbf{z}^t\mathbf{y}<\alpha$. □

Theorem 5.3 (Farkas Theorem) *Let $\mathbf{A}$ be a $m\times n$ matrix and $\mathbf{c}\in R^n$ be a vector. Then, exactly one of the following systems has a solution*:

System 1: $\mathbf{Ax}\geq\mathbf{0}$ and $\mathbf{c}^t\mathbf{x}<0$ for some $\mathbf{x}\in R^n$
System 2: $\mathbf{A}^t\mathbf{y}=\mathbf{c}$ and $\mathbf{y}\geq\mathbf{0}$ for some $\mathbf{y}\in R^m$

Proof

1. Suppose that System 2 has a solution; that is, there exists a $\mathbf{y}\in R^m$ and $\mathbf{y}\geq\mathbf{0}$ such that $\mathbf{A}^t\mathbf{y}=\mathbf{c}$. Then, if for any $\mathbf{x}\in R^n$ such that $\mathbf{Ax}\geq\mathbf{0}$, then $\mathbf{c}^t\mathbf{x}=\mathbf{y}^t\mathbf{Ax}\geq 0$; that is, System 1 has no solution.
2. Suppose System 2 has no solution. Form the set $S=\{\mathbf{x}':\mathbf{x}'=\mathbf{A}^t\mathbf{y},\mathbf{y}\geq\mathbf{0}\}$. Note that the set S is a closed convex set: Let $\mathbf{x}_1,\mathbf{x}_2\in S$ and $\beta\in[0,1]$. Then there must exist $\mathbf{y}_1,\mathbf{y}_2\geq\mathbf{0}$ such that $\mathbf{x}_1=\mathbf{A}^t\mathbf{y}_1$ and $\mathbf{x}_2=\mathbf{A}^t\mathbf{y}_2$. Also, $\beta\mathbf{x}_1+(1-\beta)\mathbf{x}_2=\beta\mathbf{A}^t\mathbf{y}_1+(1-\beta)\mathbf{A}^t\mathbf{y}_2=\mathbf{A}^t[\beta\mathbf{y}_1+(1-\beta)\mathbf{y}_2]\geq\mathbf{0}$ where $\beta\mathbf{y}_1+(1-\beta)\mathbf{y}_2\geq\mathbf{0}$.

Since $\mathbf{c} \notin S$, by Theorem 5.2, there exists a nonzero vector $\mathbf{z} \in R^n$ and a scalar α such that $\mathbf{z}^t\mathbf{c} < \alpha$ and $\mathbf{z}^t\mathbf{x}' \geq \alpha$ for each $\mathbf{x}' \in S$. Because $\mathbf{0} \in S$, $\alpha \leq \mathbf{z}^t\mathbf{0} = 0$. $\alpha \leq \mathbf{z}^t\mathbf{x}' = \mathbf{z}^t\mathbf{A}^t\mathbf{y} = \mathbf{y}^t\mathbf{A}\mathbf{z}$ for each $\mathbf{y} \geq \mathbf{0}$. Since $\mathbf{y}$ can be made arbitrarily large and α is a fixed number, we must have $\mathbf{A}\mathbf{z} \geq \mathbf{0}$. We have therefore constructed a vector $\mathbf{z} \in R^n$ such that $\mathbf{A}\mathbf{z} \geq \mathbf{0}$ and $\mathbf{z}^t\mathbf{c} < 0$, i.e., System 1 has a solution. □

Theorem 5.4 (Gordan Theorem or the Arbitrage Theorem)[1] *Let* $\mathbf{A}$ *be an* $m \times n$ *matrix. Then, exactly one of the following systems has a solution*:

System 1: $\mathbf{A}\mathbf{x} > \mathbf{0}$ for some $\mathbf{x} \in R^n$

System 2: $\mathbf{A}^t\mathbf{p} = \mathbf{0}$ for some $\mathbf{p} \in R^m$, $\mathbf{p} \geq \mathbf{0}$, $\mathbf{e}^t\mathbf{p} = 1$ where $\mathbf{e} = \begin{bmatrix} 1 \\ 1 \\ \cdot \\ \cdot \\ 1 \end{bmatrix}$

Proof

1. Suppose that System 1 has a solution: $\mathbf{A}\mathbf{x} > \mathbf{0}$ for some $\mathbf{x} \in R^n$. Then, we can construct a negative scalar $\delta < 0$ and a vector $\mathbf{e} = \begin{bmatrix} 1 \\ 1 \\ \cdot \\ \cdot \\ 1 \end{bmatrix}$ such that $\mathbf{A}\mathbf{x} + \delta\mathbf{e} \geq \mathbf{0}$, or $[\mathbf{A} \quad \mathbf{e}]\begin{bmatrix} \mathbf{x} \\ \delta \end{bmatrix} \geq \mathbf{0}$ and $[0\ 0 \ldots 0\ 1]\begin{bmatrix} \mathbf{x} \\ \delta \end{bmatrix} = \delta < 0$. Define $[\mathbf{A} \quad \mathbf{e}] = \mathbf{A}'$, $\begin{bmatrix} \mathbf{x} \\ \delta \end{bmatrix} = \mathbf{x}'$, and $[0\ 0 \ldots 0\ 1] = \mathbf{c}^t$. We have $\mathbf{A}'\mathbf{x}' \geq \mathbf{0}$, $\mathbf{c}^t\mathbf{x}' < 0$ and $\mathbf{x}' \in R^{n+1}$; that is, System 1 of Theorem 5.3 has a solution.
2. With the same definitions, System 2 of Theorem 5.3 can be interpreted as: There exists a vector $\mathbf{p} \geq \mathbf{0}$ and $\mathbf{p} \in R^m$ such that $(\mathbf{A}')^t\mathbf{p} = \mathbf{c}$. That is, $\begin{bmatrix} \mathbf{A}^t \\ \mathbf{e}^t \end{bmatrix} \mathbf{p} = \begin{bmatrix} 0 \\ 0 \\ \cdot \\ \cdot \\ 0 \\ 1 \end{bmatrix}$, or $\mathbf{A}^t\mathbf{p} = \mathbf{0}$ and $\mathbf{e}^t\mathbf{p} = 1$ (i.e., $\sum_{i=1}^m p_i = 1$). □

In the finance literature, the vector $\mathbf{p}$ in System 2 of the Arbitrage Theorem is termed as the risk neutral probability measure, where p_i, $i = 1, \ldots, m$, can be interpreted as the current price of one dollar received at the end of period if state i occurs. If the matrix $\mathbf{A}$ has rank m (i.e., the matrix has m independent rows), the risk

[1] See also Bazaraa et al. (1993, p. 47).

neutral probability measure $\mathbf{p}$ will be unique. m independent rows of $\mathbf{A}$ also means a complete market, i.e., every asset can be replicated by other m assets.[2] I now use the following two examples to exemplify these results.

Example 5.1 Arbitrage and Risk-Neutral Probabilities.

Assume a one-period, two states of nature world with no transaction costs. There are a money market (Security 1) which provides $1 + 0.25$ dollars at time one if one dollar is invested at time 0 (i.e., the risk-free interest rate is $r = 0.25$), and two other securities (Security 2 and Security 3) with current prices \$4 and \$500, respectively, which at time 1 provide:

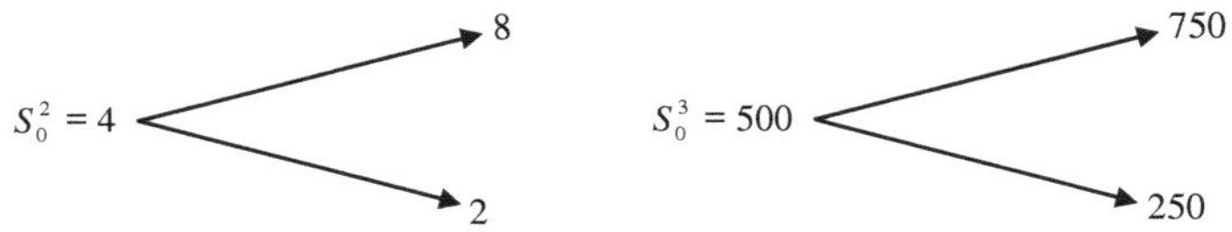

Security 2 Security 3

That is, at time one, when Security 2 provides \$8, Security 3 will provide \$750; and when Security 2 provides \$2, Security 3 will provide \$250. In this case, the two securities are not governed by the same risk neutral probability measure (i.e., System 2 of the Arbitrage Theorem has no solution):

$$\begin{cases} \text{Security 1:} \quad S_0^1 = 1 = \frac{1}{1+0.25}(\pi \times 1.25 + (1-\pi) \times 1.25); \\ \text{Security 2:} \quad S_0^2 = 4 = \frac{1}{1+0.25}\left(\frac{1}{2} \times 8 + \frac{1}{2} \times 2\right); \quad \mathbf{p}' = \begin{bmatrix} \pi' \\ 1-\pi' \end{bmatrix} = \begin{bmatrix} 1/2 \\ 1/2 \end{bmatrix} \\ \text{Security 3:} \quad S_0^3 = 500 = \frac{1}{1+0.25}\left(\frac{3}{4} \times 750 + \frac{1}{4} \times 250\right); \quad \mathbf{p}'' = \begin{bmatrix} \pi'' \\ 1-\pi'' \end{bmatrix} = \begin{bmatrix} 3/4 \\ 1/4 \end{bmatrix} \end{cases}$$

i.e., we cannot find a vector $\mathbf{p} = \begin{bmatrix} \pi \\ 1-\pi \end{bmatrix}$, $0 \leq \pi \leq 1$, such that System 2 holds:

$$\begin{bmatrix} 1.25 - 1(1+0.25) & 1.25 - 1(1+0.25) \\ 8 - 4(1+0.25) & 2 - 4(1+0.25) \\ 750 - 500(1+0.25) & 250 - 500(1+0.25) \end{bmatrix} \begin{bmatrix} \pi \\ 1-\pi \end{bmatrix} \neq \begin{bmatrix} 0 \\ 0 \\ 0 \end{bmatrix}.$$

[2] In incomplete markets, assets may not be replicated, but with no arbitrage (i.e., System 2 of Theorem 5.4 has a solution), they are still priced by the same (which may not be unique) risk neutral probability measure. See Appendix A.

By System 1 of the Arbitrage Theorem, there must exist arbitrage strategies: e.g., at time 0, we can short sell one share of Security 3, buy 60 shares of Security 2 and invest \$260(= 500 − 4 × 60) in the money market, and at time 1 we can get net profit:

$$\begin{bmatrix} 1.25-1(1+0.25) & 8-4(1+0.25) & 750-500(1+0.25) \\ 1.25-1(1+0.25) & 2-4(1+0.25) & 250-500(1+0.25) \end{bmatrix} \begin{bmatrix} x_1 \\ 60 \\ -1 \end{bmatrix}$$
$$= \begin{bmatrix} 55 \\ 195 \end{bmatrix} > \begin{bmatrix} 0 \\ 0 \end{bmatrix}.$$

When investors adopt this strategy, the time-0 price of Security 2 will go up and that of Security 3 will go down. In equilibrium (with no arbitrage), the time-0 prices of the two securities will adjust to the point that they all are priced by the same risk neutral probability measure, say, $\mathbf{p} = \begin{bmatrix} 2/3 \\ 1/3 \end{bmatrix}$,

$$\begin{cases} \text{Money Market (Security 1):} & S_0^1 = 1 = \frac{1}{1+0.25}\left(\frac{2}{3}\times 1.25 + \frac{1}{3}\times 1.25\right) \\ \text{Security 2:} & S_0^2 = 4.8 = \frac{1}{1+0.25}\left(\frac{2}{3}\times 8 + \frac{1}{3}\times 2\right) \\ \text{Security 3:} & S_0^3 = 466\frac{2}{3} = \frac{1}{1+0.25}\left(\frac{2}{3}\times 750 + \frac{1}{3}\times 250\right) \end{cases}$$

or

$$\begin{bmatrix} 1.25-1(1+0.25) & 1.25-1(1+0.25) \\ 8-4.8(1+0.25) & 2-4.8(1+0.25) \\ 750-466\frac{2}{3}(1+0.25) & 250-466\frac{2}{3}(1+0.25) \end{bmatrix} \begin{bmatrix} 2/3 \\ 1/3 \end{bmatrix} = \begin{bmatrix} 0 \\ 0 \\ 0 \end{bmatrix}.$$

Since, in the above equation, the rank of the matrix is 2 (which equals the number of the states of the nature), the market is complete, and the risk-neutral probability measure $\begin{bmatrix} 2/3 \\ 1/3 \end{bmatrix}$ must be unique. Also, any security can be replicated by other two assets:

1. Replicate Security 2's time-1 payment: At time 0, spend \$4.8 (or short-sell one share of Security 2) to buy $n = 0.012$ shares of Security 3 and borrow \$0.8(= $466\frac{2}{3} \times 0.012 - 4.8$) from the money market, and at time 1, we can get:

$$\begin{cases} \$8 = 750 \times n + (1+0.25)(4.8 - 466\frac{2}{3}\times n) & \text{if the time} - 1 \text{ price of Security 3 is } \$750 \\ \$2 = 250 \times n + (1+0.25)(4.8 - 466\frac{2}{3}\times n) & \text{if the time} - 1 \text{ price of Security 3 is } \$250 \end{cases}$$

2. Replicate Security 3's time-1 payment: At time 0, spend $\$466\frac{2}{3}$ (or short-sell one share of Security 3) to buy $n = 250/3$ shares of Security 2 and deposit $\$66\frac{2}{3}(= 466\frac{2}{3} - 4.8 \times \frac{250}{3})$ in the money market, and at time 1, we can get:

$$\begin{cases} \$750 = 8 \times n + (1 + 0.25)(466\frac{2}{3} - 4.8 \times n) & \text{if the time} - 1 \text{ price of Security 3 is } \$8 \\ \$250 = 2 \times n + (1 + 0.25)(466\frac{2}{3} - 4.8 \times n) & \text{if the time} - 1 \text{ price of Security 3 is } \$2 \end{cases}$$

Example 5.2 Contracts are European Options for One Another.

Assume a one-period, two states of nature world with no transaction costs. There already exists two assets: a money market with the risk-free interest rate $r = 0.25$, and a contract (Contract A) with time-0 price \$10, which at time-1 is worth \$16 if the economy growth rate is more than 3 % and \$6 if the growth rate is less or equal to 3 %. Now, suppose that another contract (Contract B) promises at time-1 to pay \$60 if the growth rate is more than 3 %, and \$20 if the growth rate is less or equal to 3 %. Then, what will the time-0 price of Contract B be?

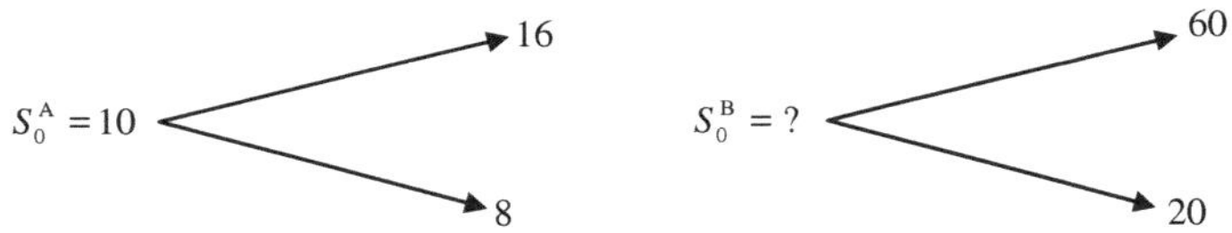

Contract A Contract B

The money market's time-1 payment vector $\begin{bmatrix} 1.25 \\ 1.25 \end{bmatrix}$ and Contract A's time-1 payment vector $\begin{bmatrix} 16 \\ 8 \end{bmatrix}$ are linearly independent, and the number of the linearly independent vectors equals the number of the states of the nature. Hence, by System 2 of the Arbitrage Theorem, the market is complete, and with no arbitrage, there exists a unique risk-neutral probability measure $\mathbf{p} = \begin{bmatrix} 9/16 \\ 7/16 \end{bmatrix}$:

$$\begin{cases} \text{Money Market:} & S_0^1 = 1 = \frac{1}{1+0.25}\left(\frac{9}{16} \times 1.25 + \frac{7}{16} \times 1.25\right) \\ \text{Contract A:} & S_0^2 = 10 = \frac{1}{1+0.25}\left(\frac{9}{16} \times 16 + \frac{7}{16} \times 8\right) \end{cases}$$

or

$$\begin{bmatrix} 1.25 - 1(1 + 0.25) & 1.25 - 1(1 + 0.25) \\ 16 - 10(1 + 0.25) & 8 - 10(1 + 0.25) \end{bmatrix} \begin{bmatrix} 9/16 \\ 7/16 \end{bmatrix} = \begin{bmatrix} 0 \\ 0 \end{bmatrix}.$$

Contract B's time-0 price is $S_0^B = 34$, i.e.,

$$\begin{cases} \text{Money Market:} & S_0^1 = 1 = \frac{1}{1+0.25}\left(\frac{9}{16} \times 1.25 + \frac{7}{16} \times 1.25\right) \\ \text{Contract A:} & S_0^A = 10 = \frac{1}{1+0.25}\left(\frac{9}{16} \times 16 + \frac{7}{16} \times 8\right) \\ \text{Contract B:} & S_0^B = 34 = \frac{1}{1+0.25}\left(\frac{9}{16} \times 60 + \frac{7}{16} \times 20\right) \end{cases} \tag{5.1}$$

or

$$\begin{bmatrix} 1.25 - 1(1+0.25) & 1.25 - 1(1+0.25) \\ 16 - 10(1+0.25) & 8 - 10(1+0.25) \\ 60 - 34(1+0.25) & 20 - 34(1+0.25) \end{bmatrix} \begin{bmatrix} 9/16 \\ 7/16 \end{bmatrix} = \begin{bmatrix} 0 \\ 0 \\ 0 \end{bmatrix}.$$

Equation (5.1) can also be written as:

$$\begin{cases} \text{Money Market:} & S_0^1 = 1 = \frac{1}{1+0.25}\left(\frac{9}{16} \times 1.25 + \frac{7}{16} \times 1.25\right) \\ \text{Contract A:} & S_0^A = 10 = \frac{1}{1+0.25}\left(\frac{9}{16} \times (60-44) + \frac{7}{16} \times (20-12)\right) \\ \text{Contract B:} & S_0^B = 34 = \frac{1}{1+0.25}\left(\frac{9}{16} \times (76-16) + \frac{7}{16} \times (28-8)\right) \end{cases} \tag{5.1'}$$

That is, Contract A can be shown as a European call option $c = \$10$ for Contract B, where the exercise price K is \$44 if the time-1 price of Contract B is \$60, and \$12 if the time-1 price of Contract B is \$20. Contract B, on the other hand, can be shown as a European put option $p = \$34$ for Contract A, where the exercise price K is \$76 if the time-1 price of Contract A is \$16, and \$28 if the time-1 price of Contract A is \$8.

5.2 Properties of the Binomial Option Pricing Model

In Chap. 4, I have derived the model-free option prices properties. In this section, I use the Arbitrage Theorem to examine the properties of the binomial option pricing model.

Assume a one-period, two states of nature world with no transaction costs. There are a money market with the risk-free interest rate r, and an asset (a stock) with time-0 price S_0 which at time-1 provides $S_0 \cdot u(u > 1)$ if the economy is good, and $S_0 \cdot d(0 \leq d < 1)$ if the economy is bad. The money market's time-1 payment vector $\begin{bmatrix} 1+r \\ 1+r \end{bmatrix}$ and the stock's time-1 payment vector $\begin{bmatrix} S_0 u \\ S_0 d \end{bmatrix}$ are linearly independent, and the number of the linearly independent vectors equals the number of the states of the nature. Hence, by System 2 of the Arbitrage Theorem, the market is complete, and with no arbitrage, there exists a unique risk-neutral probability measure

$\mathbf{p} = \begin{bmatrix} \pi \\ 1 - \pi \end{bmatrix}$. Suppose also that there are one European call option and one European put option based on the same stock with exercise price K:

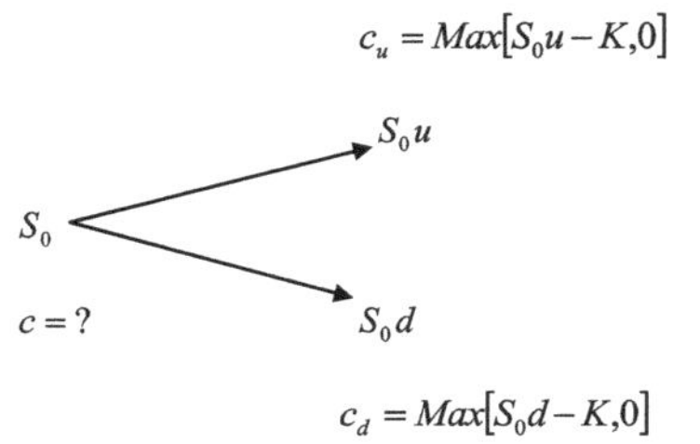

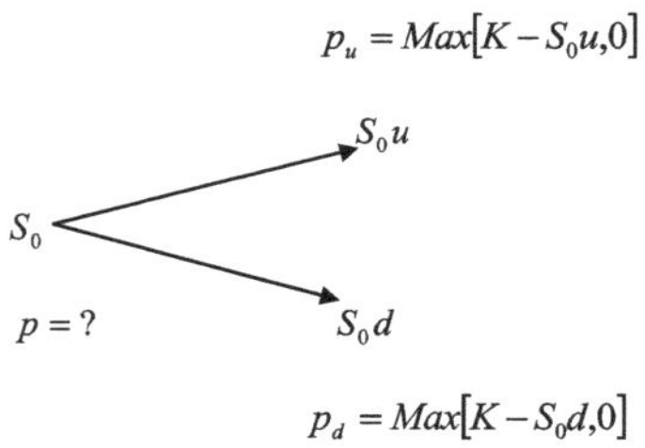

By System 2 of the Arbitrage Theorem, the prices of these assets are:

$$\begin{cases} \text{Money Market (Security 1):} & 1 = \frac{1}{1+r}[\pi(1+r) + (1-\pi)(1+r)] \\ \text{Asset (Security 2):} & S_0 = \frac{1}{1+r}[\pi \cdot S_0u + (1-\pi) \cdot S_0d] \\ \text{Security 3:} & c = \frac{1}{1+r}[\pi \cdot Max(S_0u - K, 0) + (1-\pi) \cdot Max(S_0d - K, 0)] \\ \text{Security 4:} & p = \frac{1}{1+r}[\pi \cdot Max(K - S_0u, 0) + (1-\pi) \cdot Max(K - S_0d, 0)] \end{cases} \tag{5.2}$$

From Eq. (5.2), we can derive the following properties for $S_0u > K > S_0d$.[3]

Property 5.1 *Put-Call Parity.*

$$\begin{aligned} S_0 + p &= \frac{1}{1+r}[\pi \cdot S_0u + (1-\pi) \cdot S_0d] + \frac{1}{1+r}[(1-\pi) \cdot (K - S_0d)] \\ &= \frac{1}{1+r}[\pi \cdot (S_0u - K)] + \frac{K}{1+r} = c + \frac{K}{1+r}. \end{aligned}$$

Property 5.2

$$\begin{aligned} c &= \frac{1}{1+r}[\pi \cdot (S_0u - K)] = \frac{1}{1+r}[\pi \cdot S_0u + (1-\pi) \cdot S_0d] \\ &\quad + \frac{-1}{1+r}(1-\pi) \cdot S_0d + \frac{-1}{1+r}\pi \cdot K \\ &= S_0 - \frac{1}{1+r}[\pi \cdot K + (1-\pi) \cdot S_0d] > S_0 - \frac{1}{1+r}[\pi \cdot K + (1-\pi) \cdot K] \\ &= S_0 - \frac{K}{1+r} > S_0 - K. \end{aligned}$$

---

[3] For $S_0u > S_0d > K$, $c = S_0 - \frac{K}{1+r}$ and $p = 0$. For $K > S_0u > S_0d$, $p = \frac{K}{1+r} - S_0$ and $c = 0$.

This indicates that for any American call option C, even if $S_0 - K > 0$, *it won't be exercised.*

Property 5.3

$$\begin{aligned} p &= \frac{1}{1+r}[(1-\pi)(K - S_0 d)] = \frac{-1}{1+r}[\pi \cdot S_0 u + (1-\pi)\cdot S_0 d] \\ &+ \frac{1}{1+r}(1-\pi)\cdot K + \frac{1}{1+r}\pi \cdot S_0 u \\ &= -S_0 + \frac{1}{1+r}[\pi \cdot S_0 u + (1-\pi)K] > -S_0 \\ &+ \frac{1}{1+r}[\pi \cdot K + (1-\pi)\cdot K] = \frac{K}{1+r} - S_0 \end{aligned}$$

Property 5.4 *Suppose* $c = p$, *i.e.,* $\frac{1}{1+r}[\pi \cdot (S_0 u - K)] = \frac{1}{1+r}[(1-\pi)(K - S_0 d)]$. *Then* $K = S_0(1+r)$, *i.e., the exercise price must equal the underlying asset's forward price.*

An example could be:

$$\begin{cases} \text{Money Market (Security 1):} & S_0^1 = 1 = \frac{1}{1+0.25}\left(\frac{3}{4}\times 1.25 + \frac{1}{4}\times 1.25\right) \\ \text{Security 2:} & S_0^2 = 48 = \frac{1}{1+0.25}\left(\frac{3}{4}\times 75 + \frac{1}{4}\times 15\right) \\ \text{Security 3:} & S_0^3 = 68 = \frac{1}{1+0.25}\left(\frac{3}{4}\times 100 + \frac{1}{4}\times 40\right) \\ \text{Security 4:} & c = 9 = \frac{1}{1+0.25}\left(\frac{3}{4}\times (75-60)\right) = \frac{1}{1+0.25}\left(\frac{3}{4}\times (100-85)\right) \\ \text{Security 5:} & p = 9 = \frac{1}{1+0.25}\left(\frac{1}{4}\times (60-15)\right) = \frac{1}{1+0.25}\left(\frac{1}{4}\times (85-40)\right) \end{cases}$$

where the same call and put option price: $c = p = \$9$ *can be dependent on Security 2* (S_0^2) *with* $K = S_0^2(1+r) = 48(1+0.25) = \$60$, *or dependent on Security 3* (S_0^3) *with* $K = S_0^3(1+r) = 68(1+0.25) = \$85$.

Property 5.5.1 *Let* $\Delta K = K' - K > 0$, *Then*

$$\begin{aligned} \Delta c = c' - c &= \frac{1}{1+r}[\pi \cdot (S_0 u - K')] - \frac{1}{1+r}[\pi \cdot (S_0 u - K)] \\ &= \frac{-1}{1+r}[\pi \cdot (K' - K)] < 0, \end{aligned}$$

i.e., $\frac{\Delta c}{\Delta K} < 0$, *and* $|\Delta c| < \left|\frac{\Delta K}{1+r}\right|$ *because* $r > 0$ *and* $0 < \pi < 1$;

$$\begin{aligned} \Delta p = p' - p &= \frac{1}{1+r}[(1-\pi)\cdot (K' - S_0 d)] - \frac{1}{1+r}[(1-\pi)\cdot (K - S_0 d)] \\ &= \frac{1}{1+r}[(1-\pi)\cdot (K' - K)] > 0, \end{aligned}$$

i.e., $\frac{\Delta p}{\Delta K} > 0$, *and* $|\Delta p| < \left|\frac{\Delta K}{1+r}\right|$ *because* $r > 0$ *and* $0 < \pi < 1$.

Property 5.5.2 $\frac{\Delta c}{\Delta r} > 0$ *and* $\frac{\Delta p}{\Delta r} < 0$.

$$S_0 = \frac{1}{1+r}[\pi(S_0 \cdot u) + (1-\pi)(S_0 \cdot d)], \; S_0 = \frac{1}{1+r'}[\pi'(S_0 \cdot u) + (1-\pi')(S_0 \cdot d)]$$

and

$$\pi' = \frac{(1+r')-d}{u-d} > \frac{(1+r)-d}{u-d} = \pi \quad \text{if} \quad r' > r.$$

With $c = \frac{1}{1+r}[\pi(S_0 \cdot u - K)]$ *and* $c' = \frac{1}{1+r'}[\pi'(S_0 \cdot u - K)]$, *we have:*

$$\frac{c'}{c} = \frac{\frac{1+r}{(1+r)-d}}{\frac{1+r'}{(1+r')-d}} > 1 \quad \text{if} \;\; r' > r; \; \frac{c'}{c} = \frac{\frac{1+r}{(1+r)-d}}{\frac{1+r'}{(1+r')-d}} < 1 \quad \text{if} \;\; r' < r, \text{ and } \frac{\Delta c}{\Delta r} > 0.$$

With $p = \frac{1}{1+r}[(1-\pi)(K - S_0 \cdot d)]$ *and* $p' = \frac{1}{1+r'}[(1-\pi')(K - S_0 \cdot d)]$, *we have:*

$$\frac{p'}{p} = \frac{\frac{1+r}{u-(1+r)}}{\frac{1+r'}{u-(1+r')}} < 1 \quad \text{if} \;\; r' > r; \; \frac{p'}{p} = \frac{\frac{1+r}{u-(1+r)}}{\frac{1+r'}{u-(1+r')}} > 1 \quad \text{if} \;\; r' < r, \text{ and } \frac{\Delta p}{\Delta r} < 0.$$

Property 5.5.3 $\frac{\Delta c}{\Delta S_0} > 0$ *and* $\frac{\Delta p}{\Delta S_0} < 0$.

Suppose S_0 *increases to* S' *and other factors (i.e.,* K, $S_0 d = S'd'$, $S_0 u = S'u'$, and r) *remain constant:*

$$S_0 = \frac{1}{1+r}[\pi(S_0 \cdot u) + (1-\pi)(S_0 \cdot d)], \quad S' = \frac{1}{1+r}[\pi'(S_0 \cdot u) + (1-\pi')(S_0 \cdot d)]$$

$$S' - S_0 = \frac{1}{1+r}[(\pi' - \pi)(S_0 \cdot u) - (\pi' - \pi)(S_0 \cdot d)] = \frac{1}{1+r}[(\pi' - \pi)S_0(u-d)]$$

or, $\pi' - \pi = (S' - S_0)\frac{1+r}{S_0(u-d)} > 0 \quad \text{when} \quad S' > S_0$.

With $c = \frac{1}{1+r}[\pi(S_0 \cdot u - K)]$ *and* $c' = \frac{1}{1+r}[\pi'(S_0 \cdot u - K)]$, *we have:*

$$\frac{c'}{c} = \frac{\pi'}{\pi} > 1 \text{ and } \frac{\Delta c}{\Delta S_0} = \frac{\frac{1}{1+r}[(\pi' - \pi)(S_0 \cdot u - K)]}{S' - S_0} > 0.$$

With $p = \frac{1}{1+r}[(1-\pi)(K - S_0 \cdot d)]$ *and* $p' = \frac{1}{1+r}[(1-\pi')(K - S_0 \cdot d)]$, *we have:*

$$\frac{p'}{p} = \frac{1-\pi'}{1-\pi} < 1 \text{ and } \frac{\Delta p}{\Delta S_0} = \frac{\frac{-1}{1+r}[(\pi' - \pi)(K - S_0 \cdot d)]}{S' - S_0} < 0$$

Property 5.5.4 (i) $\frac{\Delta c}{\Delta u} = \frac{\Delta p}{\Delta u} > 0$; (ii) $\frac{\Delta c}{\Delta d} = \frac{\Delta p}{\Delta d} < 0$; (iii) *If u changes to u′, d changes to d′, and other factors remain constant, then* $\Delta c = \Delta p$.

(i) Let $\Delta u = u' - u > 0$ *and other factors (i.e.,* K, d, S_0 and r*) remain constant. Then from* $S_0 = \frac{1}{1+r}[\pi(S_0 u) + (1-\pi)(S_0 d)]$, $\pi = \frac{(1+r)-d}{u-d} > \frac{(1+r)-d}{u'-d} = \pi'$. *With* $p = \frac{1}{1+r}[(1-\pi)(K - S_0 d)]$ *and* $p' = \frac{1}{1+r}[(1-\pi')(K - S_0 d)]$, *we have:* $\frac{p'}{p} = \frac{1-\pi'}{1-\pi} > 1$ *and* $\frac{p'-p}{u'-u} \equiv \frac{\Delta p}{\Delta u} > 0$.

$\frac{\Delta c}{\Delta u} = \frac{\Delta p}{\Delta u} > 0$ *can be derived from:*

$$\begin{aligned}(c'-c)-(p'-p) &= \left[\frac{\pi}{1+r}(S_0 u' - K) - \frac{\pi}{1+r}(S_0 u - K)\right] \\ &\quad - \left[\frac{(1-\pi')}{1+r}(K - S_0 d) - \frac{(1-\pi)}{1+r}(K - S_0 d)\right] \\ &= \frac{1}{1+r}[\pi'(S_0 u') + (1-\pi')(S_0 d)] - \frac{1}{1+r}[\pi(S_0 u) + (1-\pi)(S_0 d)] \\ &= S_0 - S_0 = 0.\end{aligned}$$

(ii) *Let* $\Delta d = d' - d < 0$ *and other factors (i.e.,* K, u, S_0 and r*) remain constant. Then* $1 - \pi' = \frac{u-(1+r)}{u-d'} < \frac{u-(1+r)}{u-d} = 1 - \pi$ *or* $\pi' > \pi$. *With* $c' = \frac{1}{1+r}[\pi'(S_0 \cdot u - K)]$ *and* $c = \frac{1}{1+r}[\pi(S_0 \cdot u - K)]$, *we obtain:* $\frac{c'}{c} = \frac{\pi'}{\pi} > 1$ *and* $\frac{c'-c}{d'-d} \equiv \frac{\Delta c}{\Delta d} < 0$.

$\frac{\Delta c}{\Delta d} = \frac{\Delta p}{\Delta d} < 0$ *can be derived from:*

$$\begin{aligned}(c'-c)-(p'-p) &= \left[\frac{\pi'}{1+r}(S_0 u - K) - \frac{\pi}{1+r}(S_0 u - K)\right] \\ &\quad - \left[\frac{(1-\pi')}{1+r}(K - S_0 d') - \frac{(1-\pi)}{1+r}(K - S_0 d)\right] \\ &= \frac{1}{1+r}[\pi'(S_0 u) + (1-\pi')(S_0 d')] - \frac{1}{1+r}[\pi(S_0 u) + (1-\pi)(S_0 d)] \\ &= S_0 - S_0 = 0.\end{aligned}$$

(iii) *If u changes to u′, d changes to d′ and other factors remain constant, then* $\Delta c = \Delta p$:

$$\begin{aligned}(c'-c)-(p'-p) &= \left[\frac{\pi'}{1+r}(S_0 u' - K) - \frac{\pi}{1+r}(S_0 u - K)\right] \\ &\quad - \left[\frac{(1-\pi')}{1+r}(K - S_0 d') - \frac{(1-\pi)}{1+r}(K - S_0 d)\right] \\ &= \frac{1}{1+r}[\pi'(S_0 u') + (1-\pi')(S_0 d')] - \frac{1}{1+r}[\pi(S_0 u) + (1-\pi)(S_0 d)] \\ &= S_0 - S_0 = 0.\end{aligned}$$

When both u and d change, let $(S_0u - S_0d)$ be the range. The following example (with $r = 0.25$) shows that although $\frac{\Delta c}{\Delta(range)} = \frac{\Delta p}{\Delta(range)}$, signs of $\frac{\Delta c}{\Delta(range)}$ and $\frac{\Delta p}{\Delta(range)}$ are undetermined:

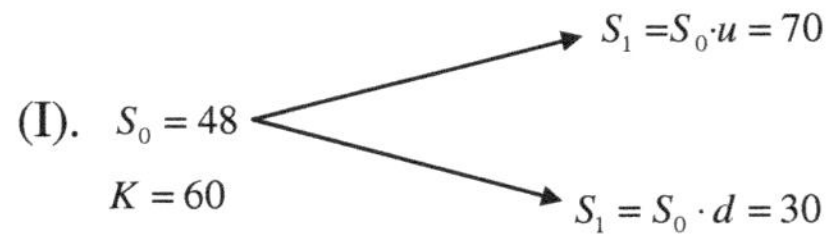

$$\begin{cases} \text{Money Market:} & 1 = \frac{1}{1+0.25}\left(\frac{3}{4} \times 1.25 + \frac{1}{4} \times 1.25\right) \\ \text{Stock:} & S_0 = 48 = \frac{1}{1+0.25}\left(\frac{3}{4} \times 70 + \frac{1}{4} \times 30\right) \\ \text{Call Option:} & C = 6 = \frac{1}{1+0.25}\left(\frac{3}{4} \times 10 + \frac{1}{4} \times 0\right) \\ \text{Put Option:} & P = 6 = \frac{1}{1+0.25}\left(\frac{3}{4} \times 0 + \frac{1}{4} \times 30\right) \end{cases}$$

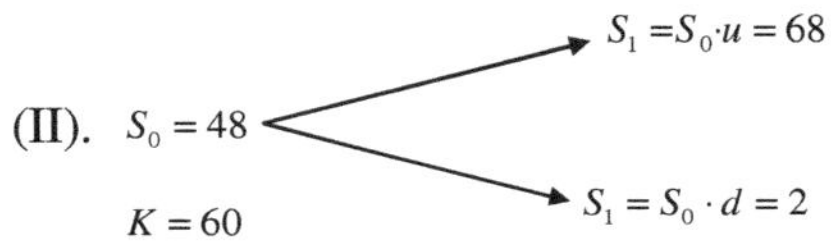

$$\begin{cases} \text{Money Market:} & 1 = \frac{1}{1+0.25}\left(\frac{58}{66} \times 1.25 + \frac{8}{66} \times 1.25\right) \\ \text{Stock:} & S_0 = 48 = \frac{1}{1+0.25}\left(\frac{58}{66} \times 68 + \frac{8}{66} \times 2\right) \\ \text{Call Option:} & C = 5.62424 = \frac{1}{1+0.25}\left(\frac{58}{66} \times 8 + \frac{8}{66} \times 0\right) \\ \text{Put Option:} & P = 5.62424 = \frac{1}{1+0.25}\left(\frac{58}{66} \times 0 + \frac{8}{66} \times 58\right) \end{cases}$$

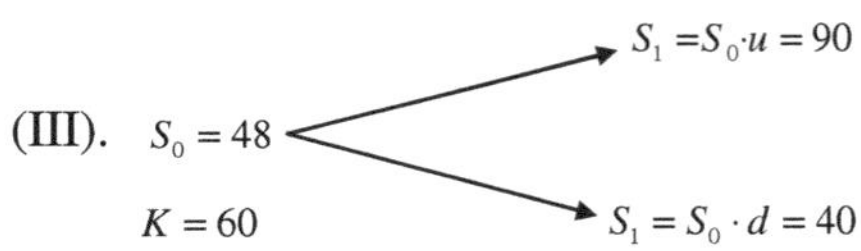

$$\begin{cases} \text{Money Market:} & 1 = \frac{1}{1+0.25}\left(\frac{2}{5} \times 1.25 + \frac{3}{5} \times 1.25\right) \\ \text{Stock:} & S_0 = 48 = \frac{1}{1+0.25}\left(\frac{2}{5} \times 90 + \frac{3}{5} \times 40\right) \\ \text{Call Option:} & C = 9.6 = \frac{1}{1+0.25}\left(\frac{2}{5} \times 30 + \frac{3}{5} \times 0\right) \\ \text{Put Option:} & P = 9.6 = \frac{1}{1+0.25}\left(\frac{2}{5} \times 0 + \frac{3}{5} \times 20\right) \end{cases}$$

We can find that the range of the stock in (II) is larger than that in (I), and (II)'s call and put prices are lower. The range of the stock in (III) is also larger than that in (I), but (III)'s call and put prices are higher. This result is different from the Black-Scholes-Merton option pricing model's $\frac{\Delta c}{\Delta \sigma} = \frac{\Delta p}{\Delta \sigma} > 0$, *where* σ *is the volatility.*

Property 5.6 *Even without changing the expiration dates, issuers of European options can adjust exercise price K to change the time value of options.*

(i) *If* $S_0 > K$, *then* $TV^p = p - Max[K - S_0, 0] = p > 0$ *and from Property* 5.2, $TV^c = c - (S_0 - K) > 0$.
Let $\Delta K = K' - K > 0$ *and* $S_0 > K'$, *we have*:

$$\Delta TV^c = TV^{c'} - TV^c = c' - (S_0 - K') - [c - (S_0 - K)] = (K' - K)\left(1 - \frac{\pi}{1+r}\right) > 0 \text{ and } \frac{\Delta TV^c}{\Delta K} > 0$$

$$\Delta TV^p = TV^{p'} - TV^p = p' - p = \frac{1}{1+r}[(1-\pi)\cdot(K' - K)] > 0 \text{ and } \frac{\Delta TV^p}{\Delta K} > 0.$$

(ii) If $S_0 < K$, *then* $TV^c = c > 0$. *Let* $\Delta K = K' - K < 0$ *and* $S_0 < K'$,

$$\Delta TV^p = TV^{p'} - TV^p = p' - (K' - S_0) - [p - (K - S_0)] = (K' - K)\left(\frac{1-\pi}{1+r} - 1\right) > 0 \text{ and } \frac{\Delta TV^p}{\Delta K} < 0$$

$$\Delta TV^c = TV^{c'} - TV^c = c' - c = \frac{-1}{1+r}[\pi \cdot (K' - K)] > 0 \text{ and } \frac{\Delta TV^c}{\Delta K} < 0$$

(iii) *For* $S_0 = K$,
if $\Delta K = K' - K < 0$,

$$\begin{aligned}\Delta TV^c &= c' - (S_0 - K') - c = (c' - c) + (K' - K)\\ &= (K' - K)\left(1 - \frac{\pi}{1+r}\right) < 0 \text{ and } \frac{\Delta TV^c}{\Delta K} > 0\end{aligned}$$

and

$$\begin{aligned}\Delta TV^p &= TV^{p'} - TV^p = p' - p\\ &= \frac{1}{1+r}[(1-\pi)\cdot(K' - K)] < 0 \text{ and } \frac{\Delta TV^p}{\Delta K} > 0;\end{aligned}$$

if $\Delta K = K' - K > 0$,

$$\begin{aligned}\Delta TV^p &= p' - (K' - S_0) - p = (p' - p) - (K' - K)\\ &= (K' - K)\left(\frac{1-\pi}{1+r} - 1\right) < 0 \text{ and } \frac{\Delta TV^p}{\Delta K} < 0,\end{aligned}$$

and

$$\Delta TV^c = TV^{c'} - TV^c = c' - c = \frac{-1}{1+r}[\pi \cdot (K' - K)] < 0 \text{ and } \frac{\Delta TV^c}{\Delta K} < 0.$$

Property 5.7 *Every non-dividend-paying asset is also a European call option and a European put option for any other non-dividend-paying asset.*

An example could be:

$$\begin{cases} \text{Money Market (Security 1):} & S_0^1 = 1 = \frac{1}{1+0.25}\left(\frac{3}{4} \times 1.25 + \frac{1}{4} \times 1.25\right) \\ \text{Security 2:} & S_0^2 = 48 = \frac{1}{1+0.25}\left(\frac{3}{4} \times 70 + \frac{1}{4} \times 30\right) \\ \text{Security 3:} & S_0^3 = 50 = \frac{1}{1+0.25}\left(\frac{3}{4} \times 75 + \frac{1}{4} \times 25\right) \\ \text{Call Option:} & c = 6 = \frac{1}{1+0.25}\left(\frac{3}{4} \times 10 + \frac{1}{4} \times 0\right) \\ \text{Put Option:} & p = 6 = \frac{1}{1+0.25}\left(\frac{3}{4} \times 0 + \frac{1}{4} \times 30\right) \end{cases}$$

where

1. *c can be a call option for Security 2 (with* $K = \$60$*) or Security 3 (with* $K = \$65$*). Also, p can be a put option for Security 2 (with* $K = \$60$*) or Security 3 (with* $K = \$55$*). This result refutes Cox, Ross and Rubinstein's* (1979) *claim that "the only random variable on which the call value depends is the stock itself. In particular, it does not depend on the random prices of other securities or portfolios*" (p. 235).
2. *One share of Security 2 is*:

   (a) *a European call option for two shares of Security 3 where* $K = \$80$ *if the time-1 share price of Security 3 is* \$75, *and* $K = \$20$ *if the time-1 share price of Security 3 is* \$25;

   (b) *a European put option for one share of Security 3 where* $K = \$145$ *if the time-1 share price of Security 3 is* \$75, *and* $K = \$55$ *if the time-1 share price of Security 3 is* \$25.

   One share of Security 3 is:

   (a) *a European call option for two shares of Security 2 where* $K = \$65$ *if the time-1 share price of Security 2 is* \$70, *and* $K = \$35$ *if the time-1 share price of Security 2 is* \$30;

   (b) *a European put option for one share of Security 2 where* $K = \$145$ *if the time-1 share price of Security 2 is* \$70, *and* $K = \$55$ *if the time-1 share price of Security 2 is* \$30.

5.3 Valuing Different Contracts

Example 5.3 Home-made Securities: A Capital Structure Irrelevancy Proposition.

Assume that in the following, the firm's capital is Security 3 which is the sum of five shares of equity:

$$\begin{cases} \text{Money Market (Security 1):} & S_0^1 = 1 = \frac{1}{1+0.25}\left(\frac{3}{4}\times 1.25 + \frac{1}{4}\times 1.25\right) \\ \text{Security 2:} & S_0^2 = 5.2 = \frac{1}{1+0.25}\left(\frac{3}{4}\times 8 + \frac{1}{4}\times 2\right) \\ \text{Security 3:} & \begin{cases} E_0^1 = 100 = \frac{1}{1+0.25}\left(\frac{3}{4}\times 150 + \frac{1}{4}\times 50\right) \\ E_0^2 = 100 = \frac{1}{1+0.25}\left(\frac{3}{4}\times 150 + \frac{1}{4}\times 50\right) \\ E_0^3 = 100 = \frac{1}{1+0.25}\left(\frac{3}{4}\times 150 + \frac{1}{4}\times 50\right) \\ E_0^4 = 100 = \frac{1}{1+0.25}\left(\frac{3}{4}\times 150 + \frac{1}{4}\times 50\right) \\ E_0^5 = 100 = \frac{1}{1+0.25}\left(\frac{3}{4}\times 150 + \frac{1}{4}\times 50\right) \end{cases} \end{cases} \tag{5.3}$$

Suppose that the fourth and the fifth shares of equity (E_0^4 and E_0^5) of the firm are changed into riskless debts (D_0^4 and D_0^5):

$$\text{Security 3:} \quad \begin{cases} E_0^{1'} = 100 = \frac{1}{1+0.25}\left(\frac{3}{4}\times \frac{500}{3} + \frac{1}{4}\times 0\right) \\ E_0^{2'} = 100 = \frac{1}{1+0.25}\left(\frac{3}{4}\times \frac{500}{3} + \frac{1}{4}\times 0\right) \\ E_0^{3'} = 100 = \frac{1}{1+0.25}\left(\frac{3}{4}\times \frac{500}{3} + \frac{1}{4}\times 0\right) \\ D_0^4 = 100 = \frac{1}{1+0.25}\left(\frac{3}{4}\times 125 + \frac{1}{4}\times 125\right) \\ D_0^5 = 100 = \frac{1}{1+0.25}\left(\frac{3}{4}\times 125 + \frac{1}{4}\times 125\right) \end{cases} \tag{5.4}$$

The market value of the firm (Security 3) at time 0 is still \$500; that is, the market value of firm is independent of its debt-equity ratio. This is just a restatement of Modigliani-Miller's first proposition.

Comparing Eq. (5.3) with Eq. (5.4), it is found that more debt means higher variance of equity's time-1 payment:

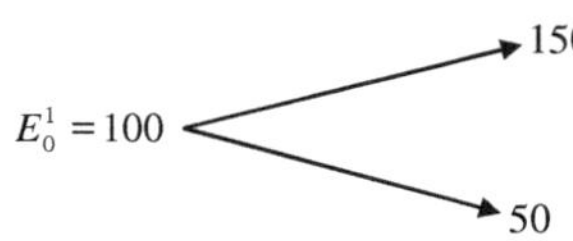

No Debt

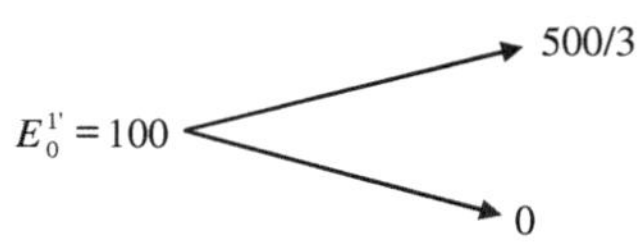

With Debt

But after the firm changes its debt-equity ratio, the equityholders can always buy only $n = 0.6$ shares of the new equity ($E_0^{1'}$) and invest \$40($=100 - 100 \times 0.6$) in the money market to re-create the time-1 payment of the old equity (E_0^1):

$$\begin{cases} \$150 = (500/3) \times 0.6 + (1 + 0.25)(100 - 100 \times 0.6) \\ \$50 = 0 \times 0.6 + (1 + 0.25)(100 - 100 \times 0.6) \end{cases}$$

or

$$\begin{bmatrix} 150 \\ 50 \end{bmatrix} = (0.6)\begin{bmatrix} \frac{500}{3} \\ 0 \end{bmatrix} + (100 - 0.6 \times 100)\begin{bmatrix} 1.25 \\ 1.25 \end{bmatrix} \tag{5.5}$$

Suppose that in Eq. (5.4), debts are risky, e.g., the risky interest rate is $\frac{7}{23}\left(= \frac{150}{115} - 1\right)$:

$$\text{Security 3:} \quad \begin{cases} E_0^{1''} = 90 = \frac{1}{1+0.25}\left(\frac{3}{4} \times \frac{450}{3} + \frac{1}{4} \times 0\right) \\ E_0^{2''} = 90 = \frac{1}{1+0.25}\left(\frac{3}{4} \times \frac{450}{3} + \frac{1}{4} \times 0\right) \\ E_0^{3''} = 90 = \frac{1}{1+0.25}\left(\frac{3}{4} \times \frac{450}{3} + \frac{1}{4} \times 0\right) \\ D_0^{4'} = 115 = \frac{1}{1+0.25}\left(\frac{3}{4} \times 150 + \frac{1}{4} \times 125\right) \\ D_0^{5'} = 115 = \frac{1}{1+0.25}\left(\frac{3}{4} \times 150 + \frac{1}{4} \times 125\right) \end{cases} \tag{5.6}$$

The market value of the firm at time 0 is still \$500. The time-0 new equity is only \$90:

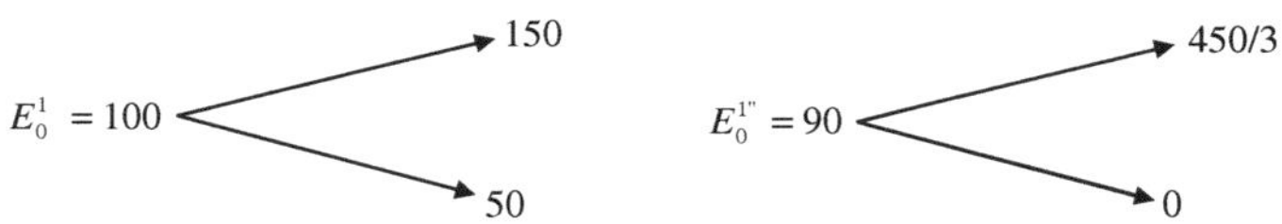

No Debt With Debt

But, after the firm changes its debt-equity ratio, the equityholders can always buy $n = 2/3$ shares of the new equity ($E_0^{1''}$) and invest \$40(=100 − 90 × (2/3)) in the money market to re-create the time-1 payment of the old equity (E_0^1):

$$\begin{cases} \$150 = (2/3)(450/3) + (1 + 0.25)(100 - (2/3) \times 90) \\ \$50 = (2/3)(0) + (1 + 0.25)(100 - (2/3) \times 90) \end{cases}$$

or

$$\begin{bmatrix} 150 \\ 50 \end{bmatrix} = \frac{2}{3}\begin{bmatrix} \frac{450}{3} \\ 0 \end{bmatrix} + \left(100 - \frac{2}{3} \times 90\right)\begin{bmatrix} 1.25 \\ 1.25 \end{bmatrix} \tag{5.7}$$

That is, after the firm changes its debt-equity ratio, the equityholders can always combine the new equity with other securities (e.g., money market) to create a "home-made equity" which will give exactly the same time-1 payment of the old equity.[4] We now have a capital structure irrelevancy proposition:

Proposition 5.1 Capital Structure Irrelevancy
In a complete market with no transaction costs and no arbitrage, changes in the firm's debt-equity ratio will not affect equityholders' wealth (welfare), and equityholders' preferences toward risk (or variance) are irrelevant.[5]

This proposition refutes the claims in the corporate finance literature that "the use of debt rather than equity funds to finance a given venture may well increase the expected return to the owners, but only at the cost of increased dispersion of the outcomes" (Modigliani and Miller 1958, p. 262); "any gains from using more of what might seem to be cheaper debt capital would thus be offset by correspondingly higher cost of the now riskier equity capital" (Miller 1988, p. 100); and "the levered stockholders have better returns in good times than do unlevered stockholders but have worse returns in bad times, implying greater risk with leverage" (Ross et al. 2012, p. 410).[6]

Example 5.4 Transferring Wealth from Debtholder to Equityholder.

In Example 5.3, assume Security 3 is a levered firm:

$$\begin{cases} \text{Money Market (Security 1):} & S_0^1 = 1 = \frac{1}{1+0.25}\left(\frac{3}{4}\times 1.25 + \frac{1}{4}\times 1.25\right) \\ \text{Security 2:} & S_0^2 = 5.2 = \frac{1}{1+0.25}\left(\frac{3}{4}\times 8 + \frac{1}{4}\times 2\right) \\ \text{Security 3:} & \begin{cases} E_0^{1''} = 90 = \frac{1}{1+0.25}\left(\frac{3}{4}\times \frac{450}{3} + \frac{1}{4}\times 0\right) \\ E_0^{2''} = 90 = \frac{1}{1+0.25}\left(\frac{3}{4}\times \frac{450}{3} + \frac{1}{4}\times 0\right) \\ E_0^{3''} = 90 = \frac{1}{1+0.25}\left(\frac{3}{4}\times \frac{450}{3} + \frac{1}{4}\times 0\right) \\ D_0^{4'} = 115 = \frac{1}{1+0.25}\left(\frac{3}{4}\times 150 + \frac{1}{4}\times 125\right) \\ D_0^{5'} = 115 = \frac{1}{1+0.25}\left(\frac{3}{4}\times 150 + \frac{1}{4}\times 125\right) \end{cases} \end{cases} \tag{5.8}$$

---

[4] Note that even before the firm changes its debt-equity ratio, the equityholders can buy 3/2 shares of the existing equity (E_0^1) and borrow \$60($=100\times\frac{3}{2}-90$) from the money market to create the time-1 payment of the new equity ($E_0^{1''}$):

$$\begin{cases} 450/3 = (3/2)(150) + (1+0.25)(90-(3/2)\times 100) \\ 0 = (3/2)(50) + (1+0.25)(90-(3/2)\times 100) \end{cases}$$

[5] After the firm changes its debt-equity ratio, the debtholders can also combine the new debt with other securities to create a home-made debt which will give exactly the same time-1 payment of the old debt (i.e., debtholders' preferences toward risk/variance are irrelevant). Thus, in complete markets, mean-variance analysis may not be meaningful.

[6] In an incomplete market, after the firm changes its debt-equity ratio, the equityholders may not be able to create a home-made equity to replicate the time-1 payment of the old equity. See Appendix B.

Suppose that the firm moves to a more uncertain project, and its time-1 payment is $\begin{bmatrix} 900 \\ 100 \end{bmatrix}$ rather than $\begin{bmatrix} 750 \\ 250 \end{bmatrix}$. Then, Eq. (5.8) becomes:

$$\begin{cases} \text{Money Market (Security 1):} & S_0^1 = 1 = \frac{1}{1+0.25}\left(\frac{3}{4} \times 1.25 + \frac{1}{4} \times 1.25\right) \\ \text{Security 2:} & S_0^2 = 5.2 = \frac{1}{1+0.25}\left(\frac{3}{4} \times 8 + \frac{1}{4} \times 2\right) \\ \text{Security 3:} & \begin{cases} E_0^{1'''} = 120 = \frac{1}{1+0.25}\left(\frac{3}{4} \times \frac{600}{3} + \frac{1}{4} \times 0\right) \\ E_0^{2'''} = 120 = \frac{1}{1+0.25}\left(\frac{3}{4} \times \frac{600}{3} + \frac{1}{4} \times 0\right) \\ E_0^{3'''} = 120 = \frac{1}{1+0.25}\left(\frac{3}{4} \times \frac{600}{3} + \frac{1}{4} \times 0\right) \\ D_0^{4''} = 100 = \frac{1}{1+0.25}\left(\frac{3}{4} \times 150 + \frac{1}{4} \times 50\right) \\ D_0^{5''} = 100 = \frac{1}{1+0.25}\left(\frac{3}{4} \times 150 + \frac{1}{4} \times 50\right) \end{cases} \end{cases} \tag{5.9}$$

It is found that when the firm moves from a more certain project (i.e., the time-1 payment is either \$750 or \$250) to a more uncertain one (i.e., the time-1 payment is either \$900 or \$100), the variance of the time-1 payment of the firm (and the variance of the time-1 payment of equity) increases, the time-0 price of equity also increases, but the time-0 price of debt decreases.[7]

Example 5.5 Pricing Convertible Bonds.

In Example 5.3, assume Eq. (5.4) where Security 3 is a levered firm. Suppose that one of the firm's riskless debts is changed into a convertible bond:

$$\text{Security 3:} \quad \begin{cases} e_0^1 = 93.75 = \frac{1}{1+0.25}\left(\frac{3}{4} \times \frac{(750-125)}{4} + \frac{1}{4} \times 0\right) \\ e_0^2 = 93.75 = \frac{1}{1+0.25}\left(\frac{3}{4} \times \frac{(750-125)}{4} + \frac{1}{4} \times 0\right) \\ e_0^3 = 93.75 = \frac{1}{1+0.25}\left(\frac{3}{4} \times \frac{(750-125)}{4} + \frac{1}{4} \times 0\right) \\ CB_0 = 118.75 = \frac{1}{1+0.25}\left(\frac{3}{4} \times \frac{(750-125)}{4} + \frac{1}{4} \times 125\right) \\ D_0^5 = 100 = \frac{1}{1+0.25}\left(\frac{3}{4} \times 125 + \frac{1}{4} \times 125\right) \end{cases} \tag{5.10}$$

Adding this convertible bond dilutes the time-0 value of one share of equity (which decreases from \$100 to \$93.75). The market value of the firm at time 0 is still \$500. The time-0 price of the option (the right) to convert a share of ordinary bond into a share of equity is (\$18.75 = 118.75 – 100).

Example 5.6 Valuing Different Types of Labor Contracts.

[7] Because the debtholders' time-1 payments have an upper bound, they will not benefit if the more uncertain project succeeds, but will suffer if the more uncertain project fails. Note that in some cases, the time-0 price of a firm may decrease when the firm moves to a more uncertain project. See Appendix C.

In Example 5.5, assume Eq. (5.10) where Security 3 is a levered firm. Suppose that the firm's hiring an additional labor (a manager) can increase its time-1 payoff from $\begin{bmatrix} 750 \\ 250 \end{bmatrix}$ to $\begin{bmatrix} 850 \\ 300 \end{bmatrix}$:

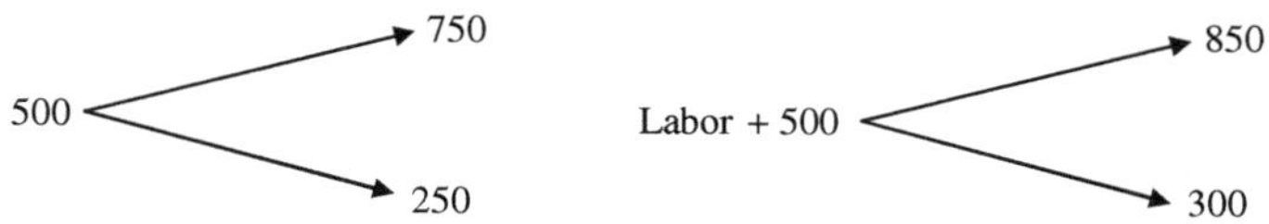

Security 3 Security 3'

The time-0 value of the whole firm will be \$570, and the time-0 value of the labor input will be \$70:

$$\begin{cases} 570 = \frac{1}{1+0.25}\left(\frac{3}{4} \times 850 + \frac{1}{4} \times 300\right) \\ 70 = \frac{1}{1+0.25}\left(\frac{3}{4} \times (850 - 750) + \frac{1}{4} \times (300 - 250)\right) \end{cases}$$

Note that different labor contractual arrangements will not affect the time-0 price of the labor input or the time-0 price of the whole capital input (which includes equity, debt and convertible bond)[8]:

Fixed-wage contract:

$$\text{Security } 3': \begin{cases} e_0^{1f} = 98.4375 = \frac{1}{1+0.25}\left(\frac{3}{4} \times \frac{(850-106.25-87.5)}{4} + \frac{1}{4} \times 0\right) \\ e_0^{2f} = 98.4375 = \frac{1}{1+0.25}\left(\frac{3}{4} \times \frac{(850-106.25-87.5)}{4} + \frac{1}{4} \times 0\right) \\ e_0^{3f} = 98.4375 = \frac{1}{1+0.25}\left(\frac{3}{4} \times \frac{(850-106.25-87.5)}{4} + \frac{1}{4} \times 0\right) \\ CB_0^{f} = 119.6875 = \frac{1}{1+0.25}\left(\frac{3}{4} \times \frac{(850-106.25-87.5)}{4} + \frac{1}{4} \times 106.25\right) \\ D_0^{5f} = 85 = \frac{1}{1+0.25}\left(\frac{3}{4} \times 106.25 + \frac{1}{4} \times 106.25\right) \\ \text{Labor}^{f} = 70 = \frac{1}{1+0.25}\left(\frac{3}{4} \times 87.5 + \frac{1}{4} \times 87.5\right) \end{cases} \tag{5.11}$$

[8] With the assumption of certainty, Cheung (1968) finds that different labor contractual arrangements will not affect the efficiency of resource allocation.

Share contract (where the labor's share: $x = 7/57$; the capital providers' share:$1 - x = 50/57$):

$$\text{Security } 3': \begin{cases} e_0^{1s} = 92.105263 = \frac{1}{1+0.25}\left(\frac{3}{4} \times \frac{850(1-x)-300(1-x)/2}{4} + \frac{1}{4} \times 0\right) \\ e_0^{2s} = 92.105263 = \frac{1}{1+0.25}\left(\frac{3}{4} \times \frac{850(1-x)-300(1-x)/2}{4} + \frac{1}{4} \times 0\right) \\ e_0^{3s} = 92.105263 = \frac{1}{1+0.25}\left(\frac{3}{4} \times \frac{850(1-x)-300(1-x)/2}{4} + \frac{1}{4} \times 0\right) \\ CB_0^{s} = 118.421052 = \frac{1}{1+0.25}\left(\frac{3}{4} \times \frac{850(1-x)-300(1-x)/2}{4} + \frac{1}{4} \times \frac{300(1-x)}{2}\right) \\ D_0^{5s} = 105.263158 = \frac{1}{1+0.25}\left(\frac{3}{4} \times \frac{300(1-x)}{2} + \frac{1}{4} \times \frac{300(1-x)}{2}\right) \\ \text{Labor}^{s} = 70 = \frac{1}{1+0.25}\left(\frac{3}{4} \times 850x + \frac{1}{4} \times 300x\right) \end{cases} \tag{5.12}$$

Mixed contract (where the labor obtains 50 dollars and has share:$y = 3/53$, and capital providers' share is: $1 - y = 50/53$):

Security $3'$:

$$\begin{cases} e_0^{1m} = 95.518868 = \frac{1}{1+0.25}\left(\frac{3}{4} \times \frac{(850-50)(1-y)-(300-50)(1-y)/2}{4} + \frac{1}{4} \times 0\right) \\ e_0^{2m} = 95.518868 = \frac{1}{1+0.25}\left(\frac{3}{4} \times \frac{(850-50)(1-y)-(300-50)(1-y)/2}{4} + \frac{1}{4} \times 0\right) \\ e_0^{3m} = 95.518868 = \frac{1}{1+0.25}\left(\frac{3}{4} \times \frac{(850-50)(1-y)-(300-50)(1-y)/2}{4} + \frac{1}{4} \times 0\right) \\ CB_0^{m} = 119.103773 = \frac{1}{1+0.25}\left[\frac{3}{4} \times \frac{(850-50)(1-y)-(300-50)(1-y)/2}{4} \right. \\ \qquad \left. + \frac{1}{4} \times \frac{(300-50)(1-y)}{2}\right] \\ D_0^{5m} = 94.339622 = \frac{1}{1+0.25}\left(\frac{3}{4} \times \frac{(300-50)(1-y)}{2} + \frac{1}{4} \times \frac{(300-50)(1-y)}{2}\right) \\ \text{Labor}^{m} = 70 = \frac{1}{1+0.25}\left(\frac{3}{4} \times (50 + (850-50)y) + \frac{1}{4} \times (50 + (300-50)y)\right) \end{cases} \tag{5.13}$$

Proposition 5.2 (Irrelevancy of Different Labor Contractual Arrangements)
In a complete market with no transaction costs and no arbitrage, different labor contractual arrangements have the same time-0 market value.

In Example 5.6, suppose that after the resource providers contributed their resources, the firm moves to a more uncertain project, and its time-1 payoff is $\begin{bmatrix} 1{,}200 \\ 40 \end{bmatrix}$ instead of $\begin{bmatrix} 850 \\ 300 \end{bmatrix}$. Assume that the labor is the first to get payment, the common bondholder is the second to get payment, the convertible bondholder is the third to get payment, and the equityholder obtains residual:

Fixed-wage contract:

$$\text{Security } 3'': \begin{cases} e_0^{1f''} = 150.9375 = \frac{1}{1+0.25}\left(\frac{3}{4}\times\frac{(1{,}200-106.25-87.5)}{4}+\frac{1}{4}\times 0\right) \\ e_0^{2f''} = 150.9375 = \frac{1}{1+0.25}\left(\frac{3}{4}\times\frac{(1{,}200-106.25-87.5)}{4}+\frac{1}{4}\times 0\right) \\ e_0^{3f''} = 150.9375 = \frac{1}{1+0.25}\left(\frac{3}{4}\times\frac{(1{,}200-106.25-87.5)}{4}+\frac{1}{4}\times 0\right) \\ CB_0^{f''} = 150.9375 = \frac{1}{1+0.25}\left(\frac{3}{4}\times\frac{(1{,}200-106.25-87.5)}{4}+\frac{1}{4}\times 0\right) \\ D_0^{5f''} = 63.75 = \frac{1}{1+0.25}\left(\frac{3}{4}\times 106.25+\frac{1}{4}\times 0\right) \\ \text{Labor}^{f''} = 60.5 = \frac{1}{1+0.25}\left(\frac{3}{4}\times 87.5+\frac{1}{4}\times 40\right) \end{cases} \tag{5.14}$$

Share contract (where labor share:$x = 7/57$; capital providers share: $1 - x = 50/57$):

$$\text{Security } 3'': \begin{cases} e_0^{1s'} = 138.157895 = \frac{1}{1+0.25}\left(\frac{3}{4}\times\frac{1{,}200(1-x)-300(1-x)/2}{4}+\frac{1}{4}\times 0\right) \\ e_0^{2s'} = 138.157895 = \frac{1}{1+0.25}\left(\frac{3}{4}\times\frac{1{,}200(1-x)-300(1-x)/2}{4}+\frac{1}{4}\times 0\right) \\ e_0^{3s'} = 138.157895 = \frac{1}{1+0.25}\left(\frac{3}{4}\times\frac{1{,}200(1-x)-300(1-x)/2}{4}+\frac{1}{4}\times 0\right) \\ CB_0^{s'} = 141.666667 = \frac{1}{1+0.25}\left(\frac{3}{4}\times\frac{1{,}200(1-x)-300(1-x)/2}{4}+\frac{1}{4}\times\frac{40(1-x)}{2}\right) \\ D_0^{5s'} = 82.45614 = \frac{1}{1+0.25}\left(\frac{3}{4}\times\frac{300(1-x)}{2}+\frac{1}{4}\times\frac{40(1-x)}{2}\right) \\ \text{Labor}^{s'} = 89.403508 = \frac{1}{1+0.25}\left(\frac{3}{4}\times 1{,}200x+\frac{1}{4}\times 40x\right) \end{cases} \tag{5.15}$$

Mixed contract (where the labor obtains 50 dollars and has share: $y = 3/53$, and capital providers' share is: $1 - y = 50/53$):

$$\text{Security } 3'': \begin{cases} e_0^{1m'} = 145.047169 = \frac{1}{1+0.25}\left(\frac{3}{4}\times\frac{(1{,}200-50)(1-y)-(300-50)(1-y)/2}{4}+\frac{1}{4}\times 0\right) \\ e_0^{2m'} = 145.047169 = \frac{1}{1+0.25}\left(\frac{3}{4}\times\frac{(1{,}200-50)(1-y)-(300-50)(1-y)/2}{4}+\frac{1}{4}\times 0\right) \\ e_0^{3m'} = 145.047169 = \frac{1}{1+0.25}\left(\frac{3}{4}\times\frac{(1{,}200-50)(1-y)-(300-50)(1-y)/2}{4}+\frac{1}{4}\times 0\right) \\ CB_0^{m'} = 145.047169 = \frac{1}{1+0.25}\left(\frac{3}{4}\times\frac{(1{,}200-50)(1-y)-(300-50)(1-y)/2}{4}+\frac{1}{4}\times 0\right) \\ D_0^{5m'} = 70.754717 = \frac{1}{1+0.25}\left(\frac{3}{4}\times\frac{(300-50)(1-y)}{2}+\frac{1}{4}\times 0\right) \\ \text{Labor}^{m'} = 77.056604 = \frac{1}{1+0.25}\left(\frac{3}{4}\times (50+(1{,}200-50)y)+\frac{1}{4}\times 40\right) \end{cases} \tag{5.16}$$

It shows that the time-0 prices of the whole firm, the equity, and the convertible bond will increase. The time-0 price of the ordinary bond will decrease. The time-0 price of the labor input will decrease if it is under the fixed-wage contract. The time-0 price of the labor input will increase if it is under the share or the mixed contracts.

These result show that when the firm moves from a more certain project to a more uncertain project, fixed-income assets suffer loss and non-fixed-income assets benefit.

Appendix A: Incomplete Market

In incomplete markets, securities may not be replicated, but with no arbitrage (i.e., System 2 of Theorem 5.4 has a solution), they are still priced by the same (which may not be unique) risk neutral probability measure. For example, assume that only two securities (one of them is a money market with interest rate $r = 0.25$) exist in a non-arbitrage, one-period, five states of nature world:

$$\begin{cases} \text{Money Market (Security 1):} & S_0^1 = \frac{1}{1+0.25}(p_1 \times 1.25 + p_2 \times 1.25 + p_3 \times 1.25 + p_4 \times 1.25 + p_5 \times 1.25) \\ \text{Security 2:} & S_0^2 = \frac{1}{1+0.25}(p_1 \times 10 + p_2 \times 8 + p_3 \times 4 + p_4 \times 2 + p_5 \times 1) \\ & p_1,\ p_2,\ p_3,\ p_4,\ p_5 \geq 0; \quad \sum_{i=1}^{5} p_i = 1 \end{cases}$$

Suppose that there is a new security: Security 3 whose time-1 payoff is: $\mathbf{c} = \begin{bmatrix} 12.8 \\ 10.4 \\ 5.6 \\ 3.2 \\ 2 \end{bmatrix}$. Because $\mathbf{c}$ lies in the subspace spanned by $\mathbf{a} = \begin{bmatrix} 1.25 \\ 1.25 \\ 1.25 \\ 1.25 \\ 1.25 \end{bmatrix}$ and $\mathbf{b} = \begin{bmatrix} 10 \\ 8 \\ 4 \\ 2 \\ 1 \end{bmatrix}$ (i.e., $\mathbf{c} \in S = \{\alpha\mathbf{a} + \beta\mathbf{b} : \ \alpha,\ \beta \in R^1\}$), the time-1 payoff of Security 3 can be replicated by those of Securities 1 and 2:

$$\begin{bmatrix} 12.8 \\ 10.4 \\ 5.6 \\ 3.2 \\ 2 \end{bmatrix} = (0.64)\begin{bmatrix} 1.25 \\ 1.25 \\ 1.25 \\ 1.25 \\ 1.25 \end{bmatrix} + (1.2)\begin{bmatrix} 10 \\ 8 \\ 4 \\ 2 \\ 1 \end{bmatrix}$$

The time-0 price of Security 3 is: $S_0^3 = (0.64)\ S_0^1 + (1.2)\ S_0^2$, and with no arbitrage, the three securities are priced by the same risk neutral probability measure:

$$\begin{cases} \text{Money Market (Security 1):} & S_0^1 = \frac{1}{1+0.25}(p_1 \times 1.25 + p_2 \times 1.25 + p_3 \times 1.25 + p_4 \times 1.25 + p_5 \times 1.25) \\ \text{Security 2:} & S_0^2 = \frac{1}{1+0.25}(p_1 \times 10 + p_2 \times 8 + p_3 \times 4 + p_4 \times 2 + p_5 \times 1) \\ \text{Security 3:} & S_0^3 = \frac{1}{1+0.25}(p_1 \times 12.8 + p_2 \times 10.4 + p_3 \times 5.6 + p_4 \times 3.2 + p_5 \times 2) \\ & = (0.64)\ S_0^1 + (1.2)\ S_0^2 \\ & p_1,\ p_2,\ p_3,\ p_4,\ p_5 \geq 0; \quad \sum_{i=1}^{5} p_i = 1 \end{cases}$$

Suppose that the time-1 payoff of Security 3 is: $\mathbf{c}' = \begin{bmatrix} 11.25 \\ 9.25 \\ 5.25 \\ 3.25 \\ 2 \end{bmatrix}$. Because $\mathbf{c}' \notin S = \{\alpha\,\mathbf{a} + \beta\,\mathbf{b} :\ \alpha,\ \beta \in R^1\}$, the time-1 payoff of Security 3 cannot be replicated by those of Securities 1 and 2. But with no arbitrage (i.e., System 2 of Theorem 5.4 has a solution), all the three securities will be priced by the same risk neutral probability measure:

$$\begin{cases} \text{Money Market (Security 1):} & S_0^1 = \frac{1}{1+0.25}(p_1 \times 1.25 + p_2 \times 1.25 + p_3 \times 1.25 + p_4 \times 1.25 + p_5 \times 1.25) \\ \text{Security 2:} & S_0^2 = \frac{1}{1+0.25}(p_1 \times 10 + p_2 \times 8 + p_3 \times 4 + p_4 \times 2 + p_5 \times 1) \\ \text{Security 3:} & S_0^{3\prime} = \frac{1}{1+0.25}(p_1 \times 11.25 + p_2 \times 9.25 + p_3 \times 5.25 + p_4 \times 3.25 + p_5 \times 2) \\ & p_1,\ p_2,\ p_3,\ p_4,\ p_5 \geq 0; \quad \sum_{i=1}^{5} p_i = 1 \end{cases}$$

where $p_1,\ p_2,\ p_3,\ p_4,\ p_5$ may not be unique.

Appendix B: Incomplete Market and Replication of Securities

In an incomplete market, after the firm changes its debt-equity ratio, the equity-holders may not be able to create a home-made equity to replicate the time-1 payment of the old equity. For example, assume that only two securities exist (where one of them is a money market with risk-free interest rate $r = 0.25$) in a no-arbitrage, one-period, five states of nature world:

$$\begin{cases} \text{Money Market (Security 1):} & S_0^1 = 1 = \frac{1}{1+0.25}(1.25 \times p_1 + 1.25 \times p_2 + 1.25 \times p_3 + 1.25 \times p_4 + 1.25 \times p_5) \\ \text{Security 2:} & S_0^2 = 4 = \frac{1}{1+0.25}(10 \times p_1 + 8 \times p_2 + 4 \times p_3 + 2 \times p_4 + 1 \times p_5) \\ & p_1,\ p_2,\ p_3,\ p_4,\ p_5 \geq 0; \quad \sum_{i=1}^{5} p_i = 1 \end{cases} \tag{B1}$$

where the risk neutral probability can be $\mathbf{p}' = \begin{bmatrix} 0.2 \\ 0.2 \\ 0.2 \\ 0.2 \\ 0.2 \end{bmatrix}$ or $\mathbf{p}'' = \begin{bmatrix} 7/90 \\ 1/5 \\ 3/5 \\ 1/10 \\ 1/45 \end{bmatrix}$ or others.

Assume that Security 2 is an all-equity firm and it plans to issue a riskless debt, e.g., a debtholder pays \$0.8 at time 0 and obtains \$1 at time 1:

By $\mathbf{p}'$, Security 2:

$$\begin{cases} E_0' = 3.2 = \frac{1}{1+0.25}(9 \times 0.2 + 7 \times 0.2 + 3 \times 0.2 + 1 \times 0.2 + 0 \times 0.2) \\ D_0' = 0.8 = \frac{1}{1+0.25}(1 \times 0.2 + 1 \times 0.2 + 1 \times 0.2 + 1 \times 0.2 + 1 \times 0.2) \end{cases}$$

or,

by $\mathbf{p}''$, Security 2:

$$\begin{cases} E_0'' = 3.2 = \frac{1}{1+0.25}\left(9 \times \frac{7}{90} + 7 \times \frac{1}{5} + 3 \times \frac{3}{5} + 1 \times \frac{1}{10} + 0 \times \frac{1}{45}\right) \\ D_0'' = 0.8 = \frac{1}{1+0.25}\left(1 \times \frac{7}{90} + 1 \times \frac{1}{5} + 1 \times \frac{3}{5} + 1 \times \frac{1}{10} + 1 \times \frac{1}{45}\right) \end{cases}$$

That is, recapitalization through issuing riskless debt does not change the market value of the firm (i.e., the time-0 price of Security 2 is always \$4), and the time-0 prices of equity and debt are independent of the risk neutral probability measure used. Also, after the firm issues riskless debt, the equityholder can always create a home-made equity by combining the new equity (E_0' or E_0'') with investing \$0.8 in the money market, which will give exactly the same time-1 payment of the old equity: $\mathbf{b} = \begin{bmatrix} 10 \\ 8 \\ 4 \\ 2 \\ 1 \end{bmatrix}$.

Suppose that the time-1 payment of the debt is risky: $\mathbf{d_1} = \begin{bmatrix} 3 \\ 3 \\ 3 \\ 2 \\ 1 \end{bmatrix}$. Then the time-1 payment of the equity is: $\mathbf{e_1} = \begin{bmatrix} 7 \\ 5 \\ 1 \\ 0 \\ 0 \end{bmatrix}$. Since $\mathbf{b} \notin S = \{\alpha \mathbf{a} + \beta \mathbf{e_1} : \alpha,\ \beta \in R^1\}$ where $\mathbf{a} = \begin{bmatrix} 1.25 \\ 1.25 \\ 1.25 \\ 1.25 \\ 1.25 \end{bmatrix}$ and $\mathbf{b} = \begin{bmatrix} 10 \\ 8 \\ 4 \\ 2 \\ 1 \end{bmatrix}$, $\mathbf{b}$ cannot be replicated by $\mathbf{a}$ and $\mathbf{e_1}$. That is, the equityholder cannot combine the new equity $\mathbf{e_1}$ with the money market to create a home-made equity to replicate the time-1 payoff of the old equity: $\mathbf{b} = \begin{bmatrix} 10 \\ 8 \\ 4 \\ 2 \\ 1 \end{bmatrix}$.

Also, with different risk neutral probability measures:

$$\text{By } \mathbf{p}', \text{ Security 2: } \begin{cases} e_0' = 2.08 = \frac{1}{1+0.25}(7 \times 0.2 + 5 \times 0.2 + 1 \times 0.2 + 0 \times 0.2 + 0 \times 0.2) \\ d_0' = 1.92 = \frac{1}{1+0.25}(3 \times 0.2 + 3 \times 0.2 + 3 \times 0.2 + 2 \times 0.2 + 1 \times 0.2) \end{cases}$$

$$\text{By } \mathbf{p}'', \text{ Security 2: } \begin{cases} e_0'' = 1.71555 = \frac{1}{1+0.25}\left(7 \times \frac{7}{90} + 5 \times \frac{1}{5} + 1 \times \frac{3}{5} + 0 \times \frac{1}{10} + 0 \times \frac{1}{45}\right) \\ d_0'' = 2.28444 = \frac{1}{1+0.25}\left(3 \times \frac{7}{90} + 3 \times \frac{1}{5} + 3 \times \frac{3}{5} + 2 \times \frac{1}{10} + 1 \times \frac{1}{45}\right) \end{cases}$$

The time-0 price of Security 2 can be the sum of e_0' and d_0'' (which equals \$4.36444 > \$4), and with no arbitrage,

$$\begin{cases} \text{Money Market (Security 1): } S_0^1 = 1 = \frac{1}{1+0.25}(1.25 \times p_1 + 1.25 \times p_2 + 1.25 \times p_3 + 1.25 \times p_4 + 1.25 \times p_5) \\ \text{Security 2: } \begin{cases} e_0' = 2.08 = \frac{1}{1+0.25}(7 \times p_1 + 5 \times p_2 + 1 \times p_3 + 0 \times p_4 + 0 \times p_5) \\ d_0'' = 2.28444 = \frac{1}{1+0.25}(3 \times p_1 + 3 \times p_2 + 3 \times p_3 + 2 \times p_4 + 1 \times p_5) \end{cases} \\ p_1, p_2, p_3, p_4, p_5 \geq 0; \quad \sum_{i=1}^{5} p_i = 1 \end{cases}$$

where the risk neutral probability can be $\begin{bmatrix} 0.12127 \\ 0.24921 \\ 0.50507 \\ 0.10445 \\ 0.02 \end{bmatrix}$ or $\begin{bmatrix} 0.10984 \\ 0.25635 \\ 0.54936 \\ 0.02445 \\ 0.06 \end{bmatrix}$ or others. If this is the case, then with no arbitrage, the time-0 price of Security 2 in Eq. (B1) will be adjusted to \$4.36444 in the first place (see also Litzenberger and Sosin 1977; Huang and Litzenberger 1988, pp. 128–129):

$$\begin{cases} \text{Money Market (Security 1): } S_0^1 = 1 = \frac{1}{1+0.25}(1.25 \times p_1 + 1.25 \times p_2 + 1.25 \times p_3 + 1.25 \times p_4 + 1.25 \times p_5) \\ \text{Security 2: } S_0^2 = 4.36444 = \frac{1}{1+0.25}(10 \times p_1 + 8 \times p_2 + 4 \times p_3 + 2 \times p_4 + 1 \times p_5) \\ p_1, p_2, p_3, p_4, p_5 \geq 0; \quad \sum_{i=1}^{5} p_i = 1 \end{cases} \tag{B1'}$$

where p_1, p_2, p_3, p_4, p_5 may not be unique.

Appendix C: More Uncertain Project and the Firm's Value

In some cases, the time-0 price of a firm may decrease when the firm moves to a more uncertain project. For example, assume a firm exists in a no-arbitrage, one-period, two states of nature world (where the risk-free interest rate is: $r = 0.25$):

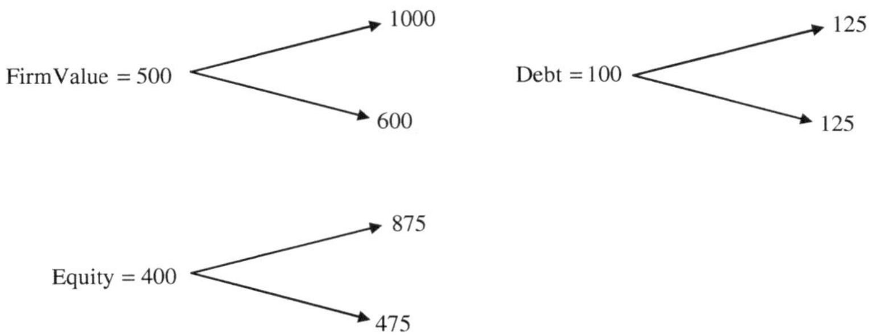

That is, the unique risk neutral probability for this world is: $\begin{bmatrix} 1/16 \\ 15/16 \end{bmatrix}$, and

$$\text{Firm value} = \begin{cases} \text{Equity:} & 400 = \frac{1}{1+0.25}\left(\frac{1}{16} \times 875 + \frac{15}{16} \times 475\right) \\ \text{Debt:} & 100 = \frac{1}{1+0.25}\left(\frac{1}{16} \times 125 + \frac{15}{16} \times 125\right) \end{cases} \tag{C1}$$

Suppose that the firm moves to a more uncertain project, and its time-1 payment is $\begin{bmatrix} 2000 \\ 100 \end{bmatrix}$ instead of $\begin{bmatrix} 1000 \\ 600 \end{bmatrix}$. Then, the time-0 prices of the whole firm, the equity, and the debt decrease:

$$\text{Firm value} = \begin{cases} \text{Equity:} & 93.75 = \frac{1}{1+0.25}\left(\frac{1}{16} \times 1875 + \frac{15}{16} \times 0\right) \\ \text{Debt:} & 81.25 = \frac{1}{1+0.25}\left(\frac{1}{16} \times 125 + \frac{15}{16} \times 100\right) \end{cases} \tag{C2}$$

Since no one benefits, the firm will not move to this more uncertain project, and Eq. (C2) cannot hold.

References

Bazaraa M, Sherali H, Shetty CM (1993) Nonlinear programming: theory and algorithms. Wiley, New York

Black F, Scholes M (1973) The pricing of options and corporate liabilities. J Polit Econ 81:637–654

Chang KP (2012) Are securities also derivatives? Am J Oper Res 2: 430–441. doi: 10.4236/ajor.2012.23051. Also in http://ssrn.com/abstract=987522

Cheung S (1968) Private property rights and sharecropping. J Polit Econ 76:1107–1122
Cheung S (1969) The theory of share tenancy. The University of Chicago Press, Chicago
Cox J, Ross S, Rubinstein M (1979) Option pricing: a simplified approach. J Financ Econ 7:229–263
Huang C, Litzenberger R (1988) Foundations for financial economics. Elsevier Science Publishing Co., New York
Litzenberger R, Sosin H (1977) The theory of recapitalizations and the evidence of dual purpose funds. J Fin 32:1433–1455
Miller M (1988) The Modigliani-Miller propositions: after thirty years. J Econ Perspec 2:99–120
Modigliani F, Miller M (1963) Corporate income taxes and the cost of capital: a correction. Am Econ Rev 53:433–443
Modigliani F, Miller M (1958) The cost of capital, corporation finance and the theory of investment. Am Econ Rev 48:261–297
Ross S, Westerfield R, Jaffe J (2012) Corporate finance. McGraw-Hill, New York

Chapter 6
Misinterpretations of Residual Claim in Finance and Corporate Law

The corporate finance literature claims that within a firm, debt is senior to equity (or debt has first claim over equity), e.g., "debt has prior claim on the firm's assets and earnings, so the cost of debt is always less than the cost of equity" (Myers 2001, pp. 84–85). In this chapter, I will show that in the firm, though *de jure* (according to the corporate law) there might be first or residual claims, there is *de facto* no first claim between fixed-income assets and non-fixed-income assets. But the first claim among fixed-income assets can affect the market values of these assets.

6.1 De Jure Versus De Facto

Example 6.1 First Claim between Equity and Debt.

Assume that at time 0, Investor A invests \$200 and Investor B invests \$200 to buy a mountain, and at time 1, the mountain will be sold. In this case, the two investors are like two equityholders and each will receive 50 % of the time-1 value of the mountain. Now, suppose that Investor B, with Investor A's agreement, wants to receive a fixed payment, say, \$250, at time 1. Then, *de jure*, according to the corporate law, Investor B is like a debtholder who has the first claim over Investor A, the equityholder. The equityholder is thus termed as the residual claimant who bears so-called 'residual risk'.[1]

I will argue that there are three ways to show that the claim of debt's being senior to equity is *de facto* not true[2]:

[1] E.g., Fama and Jensen (1983, p. 328) argue that "the residual risk—the risk of the difference between stochastic inflows of resources and promised payments to agents—is borne by those who contract for the rights to net cash flows. We call these agents the residual claimants or residual risk bearers".

[2] See also the Robin Hood story in Chap. 1.

K.-P. Chang, *The Ownership of the Firm, Corporate Finance, and Derivatives*, SpringerBriefs in Finance, DOI 10.1007/978-981-287-353-8_6

(i) Equity and debt of a firm are like long position (i.e., buyer) and short position (i.e., seller) of a forward contract. At time 0, the equityholder spends \$200 to become the buyer of the forward contract, and the debtholder spends \$200 to become the seller of the forward contract. At time 1, the debtholder will have a stock from the firm and be obligated to sell it to the equityholder at \$250, and the equityholder will have \$250 from the firm and be obligated to use it to buy the stock.[3] In this forward contract, the debtholder is willing to sacrifice the chance of obtaining more than \$250 at the good time in order to avoid the possibility of getting less than \$250 at the bad time. The equityholder, on the other hand, is willing to take the chance (the risk) of getting less than \$250 at the bad time in order to have the opportunity of obtaining more than \$250 at the good time. Just as in any forward contract where there is no first claim and no party is going to compensate another party for bearing any sort of risk, debtholder will not compensate equityholder to have the so-called first claim or seniority.

(ii) At time 0, both the equityholder and the debtholder invest the same amount of money, \$200. If the time-1 price of the mountain is greater than \$500, the equity investment will generate more profits than the debt investment. If the price is less than \$500, the debt investment will generate more profits than the equity investment. This indicates that neither equity nor debt is a dominant investment strategy.

(iii) There is a "two-step contract" (rather than "seniority") between the equityholder and the debtholder. At time 1, first, split the value of the mountain equally between the equityholder and debtholder; and second, if the debtholder's 50 % share is more than \$250 (the upper bound), she will give out any additional money to the equityholder; and if the debtholder's 50 % share is less than \$250, the equityholder will use her 50 % share to compensate the debtholder until the equityholder's share becomes zero, or the debtholder gets \$250.

Example 6.2 First and Residual Claims among Labor, Debt and Equity.

Assume that at time 0, the resource providers of the firm are: each of the two equityholders invests \$120, the debtholder invests \$120, and the labor contributes \$120 equivalency of labor service. At time 1, the firm will be liquidated, and (if possible) the debtholder wants to have \$160, the labor wants to have \$160, and the two equityholders will get the residual.

In this case, as in Example 6.1, the equity and the debt-labor portfolio are the buyer and seller of a forward contract, and neither one is a dominant investment strategy. However, even though both the labor and the debt have the same upper bound \$160, because *de jure* (according to the law) labor input is senior to debt, the

---

[3] Here it is assumed that the time-1 price of the mountain is at least \$250, i.e., the debt is riskless. If the time-1 price of the mountain is less than \$250, say, \$180, then the equityholder will be given \$180 to exchange for the stock which has zero value.

time-0 value of labor must be greater than or equal to that of debt. For example, assume a one-period, two states of nature world with no arbitrage and no transaction costs, and Security 3 is an equity-debt firm:

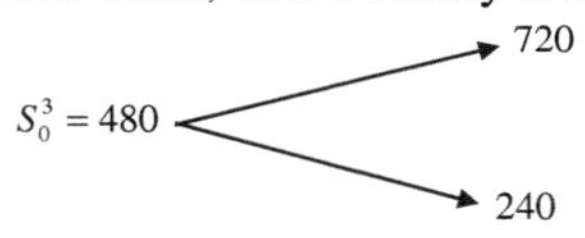

Security 3 (Firm)

$$\begin{cases} \text{Money Market (Security 1):} & S_0^1 = 1 = \dfrac{1}{1+0.25}\left(\dfrac{3}{4}\times 1.25 + \dfrac{1}{4}\times 1.25\right) \\ \text{Security 2:} & S_0^2 = 5.2 = \dfrac{1}{1+0.25}\left(\dfrac{3}{4}\times 8 + \dfrac{1}{4}\times 2\right) \\ \text{Security 3 (Firm):} & \begin{cases} E_0^1 = 120 = \dfrac{1}{1+0.25}\left(\dfrac{3}{4}\times 200 + \dfrac{1}{4}\times 0\right) \\ E_0^2 = 120 = \dfrac{1}{1+0.25}\left(\dfrac{3}{4}\times 200 + \dfrac{1}{4}\times 0\right) \\ D_0^3 = 120 = \dfrac{1}{1+0.25}\left(\dfrac{3}{4}\times 160 + \dfrac{1}{4}\times 120\right) \\ D_0^4 = 120 = \dfrac{1}{1+0.25}\left(\dfrac{3}{4}\times 160 + \dfrac{1}{4}\times 120\right) \end{cases} \end{cases} \tag{6.1}$$

Suppose that in Eq. (6.1), D_0^4 is changed into a labor input L_0^4 which at time 1 requires fixed payment \$160 and is senior to the debt D_0^3:

$$\begin{cases} \text{Money Market (Security 1):} & S_0^1 = 1 = \dfrac{1}{1+0.25}\left(\dfrac{3}{4}\times 1.25 + \dfrac{1}{4}\times 1.25\right) \\ \text{Security 2:} & S_0^2 = 5.2 = \dfrac{1}{1+0.25}\left(\dfrac{3}{4}\times 8 + \dfrac{1}{4}\times 2\right) \\ \text{Security 3 (Firm):} & \begin{cases} E_0^1 = 120 = \dfrac{1}{1+0.25}\left(\dfrac{3}{4}\times 200 + \dfrac{1}{4}\times 0\right) \\ E_0^2 = 120 = \dfrac{1}{1+0.25}\left(\dfrac{3}{4}\times 200 + \dfrac{1}{4}\times 0\right) \\ D_0^3 = 112 = \dfrac{1}{1+0.25}\left(\dfrac{3}{4}\times 160 + \dfrac{1}{4}\times 80\right) \\ L_0^4 = 128 = \dfrac{1}{1+0.25}\left(\dfrac{3}{4}\times 160 + \dfrac{1}{4}\times 160\right) \end{cases} \end{cases} \tag{6.2}$$

It is found that *de jure* the first claim (or junior claim) among fixed-income assets does affect their market values, i.e., the time-0 price of labor input is higher than that of the debt because of seniority. But the first claim among fixed-income assets has no effect on the market values of non-fixed-income assets such as equity.

Example 6.3 First and Residual Claims among Labor, Debt, Convertible Bond and Equity.

In Eq. (6.2), suppose that equity E_0^2 is changed into a convertible bond CB_0^2 which as the common debt, is *de jure* senior to the common equity E_0^1 and junior to the labor input L_0^4:

$$\begin{cases} \text{Money Market (Security 1):} & S_0^1 = 1 = \dfrac{1}{1+0.25}\left(\dfrac{3}{4}\times 1.25 + \dfrac{1}{4}\times 1.25\right) \\ \text{Security 2:} & S_0^2 = 5.2 = \dfrac{1}{1+0.25}\left(\dfrac{3}{4}\times 8 + \dfrac{1}{4}\times 2\right) \\ \text{Security 3 (Firm):} & \begin{cases} E_0^1 = 120 = \dfrac{1}{1+0.25}\left(\dfrac{3}{4}\times 200 + \dfrac{1}{4}\times 0\right) \\ CB_0^2 = 128 = \dfrac{1}{1+0.25}\left(\dfrac{3}{4}\times 200 + \dfrac{1}{4}\times 40\right) \\ D_0^3 = 104 = \dfrac{1}{1+0.25}\left(\dfrac{3}{4}\times 160 + \dfrac{1}{4}\times 40\right) \\ L_0^4 = 128 = \dfrac{1}{1+0.25}\left(\dfrac{3}{4}\times 160 + \dfrac{1}{4}\times 160\right) \end{cases} \end{cases} \tag{6.3}$$

In this case, the adding of the convertible bond CB_0^2 lowers the time-0 price of the common debt D_0^3, but it does not affect the prices of common equity E_0^1 and labor input L_0^4.

Suppose that in Eq. (6.2), half of the common debt D_0^3 is changed into a convertible bond CB_0^2:

$$\begin{cases} \text{Money Market (Security 1):} & S_0^1 = 1 = \dfrac{1}{1+0.25}\left(\dfrac{3}{4}\times 1.25 + \dfrac{1}{4}\times 1.25\right) \\ \text{Security 2:} & S_0^2 = 5.2 = \dfrac{1}{1+0.25}\left(\dfrac{3}{4}\times 8 + \dfrac{1}{4}\times 2\right) \\ \text{Security 3 (Firm):} & \begin{cases} E_0^1 = 96 = \dfrac{1}{1+0.25}\left(\dfrac{3}{4}\times 160 + \dfrac{1}{4}\times 0\right) \\ E_0^2 = 96 = \dfrac{1}{1+0.25}\left(\dfrac{3}{4}\times 160 + \dfrac{1}{4}\times 0\right) \\ CB_0^2 = 104 = \dfrac{1}{1+0.25}\left(\dfrac{3}{4}\times 160 + \dfrac{1}{4}\times 40\right) \\ D_0^3 = 56 = \dfrac{1}{1+0.25}\left(\dfrac{3}{4}\times \dfrac{160}{2} + \dfrac{1}{4}\times 40\right) \\ L_0^4 = 128 = \dfrac{1}{1+0.25}\left(\dfrac{3}{4}\times 160 + \dfrac{1}{4}\times 160\right) \end{cases} \end{cases} \tag{6.4}$$

In this case, the adding of the convertible bond CB_0^2 lowers the time-0 price of common equity E_0^1 and E_0^2. But it does not affect the time-0 price of labor input L_0^4.

6.2 Agency Costs and Residual Claim

In the above section, we have assumed zero transaction cost. In the real world, there are agency costs (e.g., gold-plating, on-the-job-consumption or shirking), and *de jure* first/residual claims may make differences. For example, in Eq. (6.4) if the agency cost of the firm (Security 3) is \$12 (i.e. opportunistic behavior results in \$12 loss), the time-0 market value of the whole firm will drop from \$480 to \$470.4 $(= 480 - 12/(1 + 0.25))$ and:

$$\begin{cases} \text{Money Market (Security 1):} & S_0^1 = 1 = \dfrac{1}{1+0.25}\left(\dfrac{3}{4}\times 1.25 + \dfrac{1}{4}\times 1.25\right) \\ \text{Security 2:} & S_0^2 = 5.2 = \dfrac{1}{1+0.25}\left(\dfrac{3}{4}\times 8 + \dfrac{1}{4}\times 2\right) \\ \text{Security 3 (Firm):} & \begin{cases} E_0^1 = 93.6 = \dfrac{1}{1+0.25}\left(\dfrac{3}{4}\times 156 + \dfrac{1}{4}\times 0\right) \\ E_0^2 = 93.6 = \dfrac{1}{1+0.25}\left(\dfrac{3}{4}\times 156 + \dfrac{1}{4}\times 0\right) \\ CB_0^2 = 100.4 = \dfrac{1}{1+0.25}\left(\dfrac{3}{4}\times 156 + \dfrac{1}{4}\times 34\right) \\ D_0^3 = 54.8 = \dfrac{1}{1+0.25}\left(\dfrac{3}{4}\times \dfrac{160}{2} + \dfrac{1}{4}\times 34\right) \\ L_0^4 = 128 = \dfrac{1}{1+0.25}\left(\dfrac{3}{4}\times 160 + \dfrac{1}{4}\times 160\right) \end{cases} \end{cases} \tag{6.5}$$

That is, the occurrence of agency cost affects not only residual claimants (the common equityholders and the convertible bondholder) but also junior claimant (the common debtholder).

If in Eq. (6.4), agency cost is bigger, say, \$96, the time-0 market value of the whole firm will drop from \$480 to \$403.2 $(= 480 - 96/(1 + 0.25))$ and:

$$\begin{cases} \text{Money Market (Security 1):} & S_0^1 = 1 = \dfrac{1}{1+0.25}\left(\dfrac{3}{4}\times 1.25 + \dfrac{1}{4}\times 1.25\right) \\ \text{Security 2:} & S_0^2 = 5.2 = \dfrac{1}{1+0.25}\left(\dfrac{3}{4}\times 8 + \dfrac{1}{4}\times 2\right) \\ \text{Security 3 (Firm):} & \begin{cases} E_0^1 = 76.8 = \dfrac{1}{1+0.25}\left(\dfrac{3}{4}\times 128 + \dfrac{1}{4}\times 0\right) \\ E_0^2 = 76.8 = \dfrac{1}{1+0.25}\left(\dfrac{3}{4}\times 128 + \dfrac{1}{4}\times 0\right) \\ CB_0^2 = 76.8 = \dfrac{1}{1+0.25}\left(\dfrac{3}{4}\times 128 + \dfrac{1}{4}\times 0\right) \\ D_0^3 = 48 = \dfrac{1}{1+0.25}\left(\dfrac{3}{4}\times \dfrac{160}{2} + \dfrac{1}{4}\times 0\right) \\ L_0^4 = 124.8 = \dfrac{1}{1+0.25}\left(\dfrac{3}{4}\times 160 + \dfrac{1}{4}\times 144\right) \end{cases} \end{cases} \tag{6.6}$$

In this case, all the resource providers (including the labor input that has *de jure* first claim) are affected.

The results in Eqs. (6.5) and (6.6) show that when there is agency cost, residual claimants will be the first affected. When agency cost becomes larger, it may affect all the resource providers though the input having the first claim may be least affected. These results also cast doubt on the claim in the literature that "owners of independent, non-firm-specific resources will not value the right of control as highly because their wealth is not affected by the firm's fortunes" (Alchian and Woodward 1987, p. 119).

6.3 Moral Hazard and Residual Claim

In the economic literature, some argue that assigning control and monitoring right to residual claimants can reduce agency costs in organizations. For example, Holmstrom (1979) and Grossman and Hart (1983) argue that the least easily monitored agent (i.e., the manager) whose effort makes the most difference to output should be the residual claimant. Klein et al. (1978) suggest that the "monitoring the monitors" problem may be solved by making the owners of the most firm-specific assets the residual claimants. Fama and Jensen (1983) propose to control the agency problems in large open corporations by separating the management (initiation and implementation by managers) and control (ratification and monitoring by shareholders) of decisions.

In the following, I will show that there will be moral hazard problems if we assign control right solely to residual claimants (no matter whether they are managers or shareholders).

Assume a one-period, two states of nature world with no arbitrage and no transaction costs, and Security 3 is a firm whose time-0 price is \$100, and time-1 payment is $\begin{bmatrix} 150 \\ 50 \end{bmatrix}$:

$$\begin{cases} \text{Money Market (Security 1):} & S_0^1 = 1 = \dfrac{1}{1+0.25}\left(\dfrac{3}{4}\times 1.25 + \dfrac{1}{4}\times 1.25\right) \\ \text{Security 2:} & S_0^2 = 5.2 = \dfrac{1}{1+0.25}\left(\dfrac{3}{4}\times 8 + \dfrac{1}{4}\times 2\right) \\ \text{Security 3 (Firm):} & \begin{cases} E_0 = 68 = \dfrac{1}{1+0.25}\left(\dfrac{3}{4}\times 110 + \dfrac{1}{4}\times 10\right) \\ D_0 = 20 = \dfrac{1}{1+0.25}\left(\dfrac{3}{4}\times 25 + \dfrac{1}{4}\times 25\right) \\ L_0 = 12 = \dfrac{1}{1+0.25}\left(\dfrac{3}{4}\times 15 + \dfrac{1}{4}\times 15\right) \end{cases} \end{cases} \tag{6.7}$$

where E_0 is the residual claimant who could be an equityholder or a manager.

Case 1 The firm moves to a more uncertain project with time-1 payment $\begin{bmatrix} 165 \\ 5 \end{bmatrix}$, and its time-0 price is still \$100:

$$\begin{cases} \text{Money Market (Security 1):} & S_0^1 = 1 = \dfrac{1}{1+0.25}\left(\dfrac{3}{4} \times 1.25 + \dfrac{1}{4} \times 1.25\right) \\ \text{Security 2:} & S_0^2 = 5.2 = \dfrac{1}{1+0.25}\left(\dfrac{3}{4} \times 8 + \dfrac{1}{4} \times 2\right) \\ \text{Security 3 (Firm):} & \begin{cases} E_0 = 75 = \dfrac{1}{1+0.25}\left(\dfrac{3}{4} \times 125 + \dfrac{1}{4} \times 0\right) \\ D_0 = 15 = \dfrac{1}{1+0.25}\left(\dfrac{3}{4} \times 25 + \dfrac{1}{4} \times 0\right) \\ L_0 = 10 = \dfrac{1}{1+0.25}\left(\dfrac{3}{4} \times 15 + \dfrac{1}{4} \times 5\right) \end{cases} \end{cases} \tag{6.8}$$

The whole firm's time-0 value does not change. But the residual claimant still benefits from transferring wealth from the debtholder and the labor.

Case 2 The firm moves to a more uncertain project with time-1 payment $\begin{bmatrix} 170 \\ 20 \end{bmatrix}$, and its time-0 price increases to \$106:

$$\begin{cases} \text{Money Market (Security 1):} & S_0^1 = 1 = \dfrac{1}{1+0.25}\left(\dfrac{3}{4} \times 1.25 + \dfrac{1}{4} \times 1.25\right) \\ \text{Security 2:} & S_0^2 = 5.2 = \dfrac{1}{1+0.25}\left(\dfrac{3}{4} \times 8 + \dfrac{1}{4} \times 2\right) \\ \text{Security 3 (Firm):} & \begin{cases} E_0 = 78 = \dfrac{1}{1+0.25}\left(\dfrac{3}{4} \times 130 + \dfrac{1}{4} \times 0\right) \\ D_0 = 16 = \dfrac{1}{1+0.25}\left(\dfrac{3}{4} \times 25 + \dfrac{1}{4} \times 5\right) \\ L_0 = 12 = \dfrac{1}{1+0.25}\left(\dfrac{3}{4} \times 15 + \dfrac{1}{4} \times 15\right) \end{cases} \end{cases} \tag{6.9}$$

The time-0 values of the whole firm and the residual claim increase. The residual claimant also benefits from transferring wealth from the debtholder.

Case 3 The firm moves to a more uncertain project with time-1 payment $\begin{bmatrix} 160 \\ 10 \end{bmatrix}$, and its time-0 price decreases to \$98:

$$\begin{cases} \text{Money Market (Security 1):} & S_0^1 = 1 = \dfrac{1}{1+0.25}\left(\dfrac{3}{4} \times 1.25 + \dfrac{1}{4} \times 1.25\right) \\ \text{Security 2:} & S_0^2 = 5.2 = \dfrac{1}{1+0.25}\left(\dfrac{3}{4} \times 8 + \dfrac{1}{4} \times 2\right) \\ \text{Security 3 (Firm):} & \begin{cases} E_0 = 72 = \dfrac{1}{1+0.25}\left(\dfrac{3}{4} \times 120 + \dfrac{1}{4} \times 0\right) \\ D_0 = 15 = \dfrac{1}{1+0.25}\left(\dfrac{3}{4} \times 25 + \dfrac{1}{4} \times 0\right) \\ L_0 = 11 = \dfrac{1}{1+0.25}\left(\dfrac{3}{4} \times 15 + \dfrac{1}{4} \times 10\right) \end{cases} \end{cases} \tag{6.10}$$

The time-0 value of the whole firm decreases, but the residual claim's time-0 value increases. The residual claimant benefits from transferring wealth from the debtholder and the labor.

The above results show that if only the residual claimants (shareholders or managers) can control the firm and determine the firm's objectives, then no matter whether the objectives of the firm increase or decrease the whole firm's market value, the residual claimants can always increase their payments at expenses of other resource providers. As discussed in Chap. 1, the firm's objectives should and will be determined by entrepreneurs who can innovate to make excess profits. Also, control and monitoring rights should be owned by all the resource providers in the firm.

References

Alchian A, Woodward S (1987) Reflections on the theory of the firm. J Inst Theor Econ 143:110–136

Fama E, Michael J (1983) Agency problems and residual claims. J Law Econ 26:327–349

Grossman S, Hart O (1983) Unemployment with observable aggregate shocks. J Polit Econ 91:907–928

Holmström B (1979) Moral hazard and observability. Bell J Econ 10:74–91

Klein B, Crawford G, Alchian A (1978) Vertical integration, appropriable rents, and the competitive contracting process. J Law Econ 21:297–326

Myers S (2001) Capital structure. J Econ Perspect 15:81–102

Index

K.-P. Chang, *The Ownership of the Firm, Corporate Finance, and Derivatives*,
SpringerBriefs in Finance, DOI 10.1007/978-981-287-353-8

MIX
Papier aus verantwortungsvollen Quellen
Paper from responsible sources
FSC® C105338

If you have any concerns about our products,
you can contact us on
ProductSafety@springernature.com

In case Publisher is established outside the EU,
the EU authorized representative is:
Springer Nature Customer Service Center GmbH
Europaplatz 3, 69115 Heidelberg, Germany

Printed by Libri Plureos GmbH
in Hamburg, Germany